Multiply Your Money

Multiply Your Money

The Easy Guide to Savings and Investments

SECOND EDITION

Nick Louth

First edition published in Great Britain in 2001. This second edition published in 2015.

Copyright © Ludensian Books Ltd

The right of Nick Louth to be identified as the Author has been asserted in accordance with the Copyright, Designs and Patents Act 1988.

Paperback ISBN: 978-0-85719-465-7
eBook ISBN: 978-0-85719-466-4

British Library Cataloguing in Publication Data
A CIP catalogue record for this book can be obtained from the British Library.

For Louise, as always

CONTENTS

ABOUT THE AUTHOR

Nick Louth has been an investment writer and a professional investor for nearly 30 years. He has been a regular contributor to the *Financial Times*, *Investors Chronicle*, *Money Observer* and numerous other publications. He is married and lives in Lincolnshire.

His website is at: **www.nicklouth.com**

Multiply Your Money was first published in 2001 by McGraw-Hill. This Harriman House edition is fully revised and updated.

Other investment titles

Funny Money

Bernard Jones and the Temple of Mammon

Dunces with Wolves

How to Double Your Money Every Ten Years (Without Really Trying)

Thrillers

Bite (an Amazon no. 1 bestseller)

Heartbreaker

CHAPTER 1.
Introduction

I N ANCIENT CHINESE LEGEND A BEGGAR WAS SHOWING A NEW GAME he had invented to the children of a small village. They enjoyed the game, which was called chess, and very soon the adults were playing too. Eventually the emperor heard of it and summoned the beggar to his palace to explain the rules. This he did, and soon the emperor too had fallen in love with the game. One day, after they had finished playing, the emperor looked up and asked: "What would you wish for, beggar man, as your reward for teaching me this marvellous game?"

The beggar man thought hard, then cleared the pieces from the chess board. "Just one grain of rice on the first square today, your Imperial Majesty."

"Just one grain of rice?"

"Yes, your Imperial Majesty, just one grain of rice on the first square. And then tomorrow two grains of rice on the second square, four on the third square the day after, and so on for two months and four days until all sixty-four squares on the board are taken."

The emperor laughed, and readily agreed, for what kind of fool was this that needed only a few handfuls of rice for such a great service?

The beggar came back to the palace every day, and the children jeered at him as he showed them the few grains of rice in the palm of his hand. By the end of the first week he brought with him a teaspoon. A week later his rice filled a wooden bowl, and a week after that he struggled with a yoke across his shoulders, groaning rice baskets suspended at each end.

The children were now silent, as were the emperor's advisors – except for the frenetic clicking of their abacuses. Only when braying at the palace gates heralded the arrival of the first of the mule trains did the emperor realise he had been duped by the beggar into losing his empire. All the rice, from all the fields and granaries across all of China, would not be enough for the last square.[1]

There is a magic in compound interest, and it can work for any of us. If each square on the chessboard is a year in your life, £10 a week invested on the first square can bring wealth of hundreds of thousands of pounds by the thirtieth or fortieth square, even with annual returns that we should expect to be around 7% rather than the 100% in the legend above.

The way to do this is to harness the engine of the economy, through the long-term ownership of shares. Many people have a couple of hundred shares from a building society demutualisation or from a privatisation, or have been left a shareholding in a will and are unsure what to do with it. Others may have never invested at all but have some savings they wish to put to work. This book will get you started, help you set your objectives and keep you away from the pitfalls that lurk for the unwary.

Of course, you don't have to own individual shares to multiply your money. There are investment funds which pool the money of thousands of people to give you the benefits of owning hundreds of

---

[1] Some bored mathematician has worked out that the number of rice grains on the last square would be eighteen trillion million, or 18,000,000,000,000,000,000, expressed more simply as 2^{63}.

different shares without having to keep track of them all. For most people, most of the time, this will be the simplest way to go. In the past such funds have tended to cream off a lot of the gains through high charges, but in recent years a breed of low-cost index trackers and exchange-traded funds (explained in chapter 10) puts almost the full power of the market right into your pocket.

For those whose investment horizon is retirement, self-invested personal pensions (SIPPs) allow you to harness the benefits of stock market growth with low charges and full tax relief. Pension types are covered in detail in chapter 4, and how to choose the right one for you is summarised briefly in chapter 5.

For many people the sheer idea of getting to grips with their finances is forbidding. Some are just starting out in their working life. Others are confronting reduced circumstances in middle age because of divorce. In chapters 6–8, *Multiply Your Money* outlines a few gradual and easy steps which anyone can make to keep track of their outgoings, turn the tables on debt, create savings and put them to work. Once you are confidently in charge of your money, never again need you dread filling out a tax return or opening a bank statement. Nor will you have to scrape together the money for a car or holiday.

Chapter 19 covers the property market and buy-to-let, another very useful way to harness the power of compound interest. For those who gather more experience, there are chapters describing how to limit risk, pick growth and value shares, and understand market cycles.

While this book does cover trading strategies, it is not intended for day-traders or those who are driven to become millionaires overnight. Common sense as well as plenty of academic research indicates that trying to second-guess the market by jumping in and out involves extra work and a lot of extra cost and is rarely worthwhile. While buying shares and never selling them is perhaps too passive in these days of rapid corporate change, it is certainly true that frenetic dealing undermines performance and peace of mind. Chapter 15 is concerned with selling gracefully, and that is what we aim to do.

I believe anyone can get very close to the market's historic average returns with less than 30 minutes' work a week. If you take a view measured in years not minutes, you never need to lose sleep over the market's day-to-day gyrations either. Chapter 14 shows how the tides of markets move month by month, never quite repeating patterns but producing variations on them. While there is never a shortage of issues to worry about – whether it is a financial crisis, inflation or interest rates – the global economy, and the companies that are its engines, will continue to generate wealth. If you want to multiply your money, you need to harness that dynamism.

For those who are willing to own individual shares, the information age is a boon. The internet has opened up free sources of research that were previously only available to market professionals. There are a variety of accounts, such as individual savings accounts (ISAs) and SIPPs, which allow us to protect the bulk of our profits against tax. Commission charges on share-trading are coming down, it is becoming easier to invest abroad, and cheap execution-only brokers are eager for our custom. Chapter 11 shows you exactly how to get started: running a dummy portfolio, researching companies, finding a stockbroker, and making your first deals.

A full explanatory glossary is included at the back of the book.

By the time you finish *Multiply Your Money* you will have the tools and confidence to take charge of your finances, build savings and multiply your money. So start early, stay with it, and have fun.

CHAPTER 2.

The Incredible Savings Machine

Introduction

I F THERE IS ONLY ONE POINT YOU TAKE OUT OF THIS BOOK, LET IT be this: if you want to stoke an investment engine that will eventually take you from modest means to being wealthy, you have to start early. The later you start, the more savings you need to put in to reach a given point.

This chapter covers just five major issues:

1. Start early, because time really is money.

2. Growth rates matter, even to the last 0.1%...

3. ... and so do costs.

4. Leave the money alone to do its work

5. Don't forget inflation.

Time is money

Anyone who has ever hired a plumber or a lawyer will know the truth in the saying 'time is money'. Put it another way: time willingly does the work of cash. Time is pretty good about this, as it does most of its work while you are asleep or getting on with your life. So do your investments a favour, give them some time to work and you can feed them less cash.

Look at Figure 2.1. This is the story of how £12,000 magically became £248,000 with the benefit of time. Alice starts at the age of 16, and pays £100 a month into a market-tracker fund. This fund manages a steady 7% a year, net of charges, which is not an unrealistic return before inflation and taxes. At the age of 26 she stops, and never puts in another penny. Importantly, neither does she ever remove a penny. Her money grows 20-fold by the time she reaches 65.

Bill, by contrast, doesn't start until he's 30. He puts in £100 a month until the day he retires, but he never catches Alice's total. His £179,000 is pretty good but he has shovelled in £43,000 to get it, nearly four times what Alice did.

Charlie starts at 40, and he too puts in £100 a month, a total of £31,200. His money is a little more than trebled by the age of 65. Not bad, of course, until he looks at Alice's stash. This may be a slightly *Alice in Wonderland* example because we are ignoring inflation, which would make Alice's early contributions costlier to provide. But the result still holds true, if not the magnitudes.

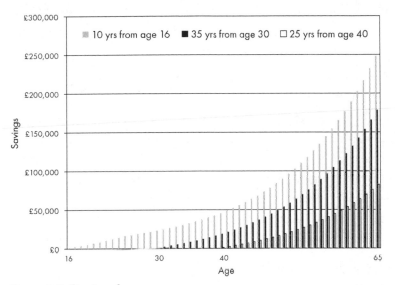

Figure 2.1: Start early

Use the magic of compound interest. The performance of three investors each returning 7% a year on their money. Alice starts at 16 and invests £100 a month for ten years. She never saves another penny, but lets it grow. Bill doesn't start until the age of 30 and puts in £100 a month until retirement at 65, while Charlie starts at 40 and invests £100 a month until retirement. At the age of 65, Alice ends up almost 40% ahead of Bill and has three times Charlie's total, yet invested only a fraction of what they did.

Long-term investment is like planting a tree. For the first few years it may look like a spindly sapling, hardly worth bothering with and not making much apparent progress even as you nurture it. Maybe you will even forget about it for a few years, then one day you look from your window and notice that what was a small acorn in your hand is now a mature tree.

Growth rates matter...and so do costs

Almost as important as starting early is getting the best return on your money that you can. Well, obviously. Let's face it, when most of us compare our bank current account statements and those for the savings account, the difference in interest income may well seem trivial. So trivial, in fact, it can often be hard to find those pennies of income among the crisp tenners you will be handing over to the bank in charges and overdraft fees.

But when it comes to the cash you put away for the very long term, small differences in interest rates matter enormously, much more than you may think. Stick £1,000 in a current account paying 1% interest when you are 20 years old, and it will not be worth £2,000 until you are 92, and what inflation would have done to it in the meantime goodness only knows. At 2% it would reach £2,000 by the time you were 56, still no big deal. But at 7% you would reach £2,000 by the age of 30, £4,000 by 40 and £8,000 by 50. Well, where you can get rates that high for so long? Only from investment.

According to the Barclays Equity Gilt Study, the British stock market has produced an annual post-inflation average return of 5.1% since 1899 – that's 114 years. That easily beats government bonds at 1.2% and savings accounts at 0.8%.[2] One absolutely essential part of this is income. You must reinvest the income from your investments – i.e. the dividends they pay out every year – to stand a chance of reaching your targets. Indeed, according to Barclays, buying £100 worth of shares in 1945 *without* reinvesting the income would have produced just £227 by 2012, after adjusting for inflation. But by reinvesting the income, that figure would have ballooned to £4,027. That's a twenty-fold improvement!

All these figures about how long cash takes to double over time have been worked out using just one simple formula:

---

2   It may be slightly confusing to use these post-inflation figures, but it is important when comparing the spending power of £1 a century ago to £1 today. To get a typical headline annual figure simply add back in typical inflation of 2%.

THE MAGIC NUMBER 72

Seventy-two is a magic number. Divide it by the percentage return on an investment and you get the number of years required to double its value. Let us say your investments returned 9.8% last year:

$$72 \div 9.8 = 7.34$$

So if you make 9.8% every year, your investments will double in just over seven years. You can also turn the formula on its head, putting in the number of years you will be investing, and find the rate required to double the value. For example, say you target doubling your savings by the time you retire, 11 years from now:

$$72 \div 11 = 6.54$$

As long as you average a return of 6.54% a year, you will make it.

A final use: money halves its value in the number of times the inflation rate goes into 72. So 2.5% inflation halves your cash in 29 years.

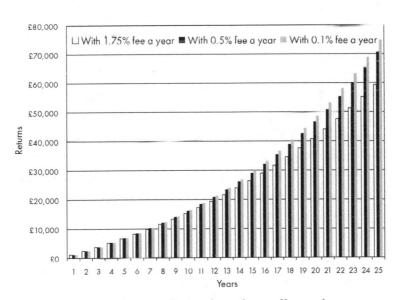

Figure 2.2: Keeping costs really low has a huge effect on long-term returns

This diagram shows the difference on a 25-year time horizon between three stock market funds to which investors contribute £100 per month. They each earn 7% a year gross, but one has a typical active fund type cost of 1.75%, another is a market tracker with a typical fee of 0.5% and one is an ultra-low cost tracker which charges just 0.1%. The difference between them is staggering.

Figure 2.2 shows that in the long term even small charges matter. The difference between 0.5% and 0.1% is worth £5,000 over 25 years. A subtle lesson to draw from this is that investors should spend more time minimising the overheads of their investments than they do seeking higher gross returns. Low costs deliver each and every day, without adding any risk to the net returns, and with no further oversight involved. That is almost never true of seeking better investment performance, which quite often involves adding risk. (For more on this see chapter 9.)

Leave the money alone

Leaving money alone pretty much speaks for itself. It isn't any good stuffing away thousands of pounds a year if every couple of years you raid that money for a holiday or a new conservatory. To do its work, the cash must be working away for the very long term, and it must be money that you know you won't need day to day. Psychologically it is much harder to get going again once you have rifled your savings, and it is harder to keep track of how well those savings are working. Deciding how much you can reasonably put away isn't easy, and is covered in chapter 8. However, once you have decided, you should do all you can to stick to it. It is better to consistently put away small amounts that you know you can afford than to overreach yourself and then have to sell something in a hurry. You can bet your bottom dollar that the times when you are most likely to need to raid your nest egg are just those times when the economy is in recession and the stock market is performing poorly. Forced sellers always lose out, because they get a poor price.

Inflation

When you consider the real value of savings into the future, you have to take account of inflation. High inflation is the great destroyer of savings, as anyone living in Germany between the first and second world wars, or in Latin America in the 1960s, can testify. But even low inflation takes quite a bite over the long term. Figure 2.3 shows a chart comparing the real, i.e. post-inflation, rates of return on shares, British government bonds (also known as gilts), and cash (deposit accounts).

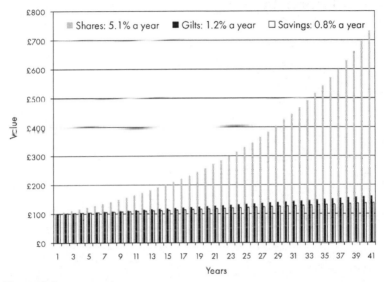

Figure 2.3

Forty years of real compounded investment at average historic rates for equities, gilts and savings (data from Barclays Equity Gilt study 2014).

More than a hundred years of experience shows that inflation consumes almost all the return from low-yield investments. Money invested in shares, however, still grows substantially in real terms.

Conclusion

We all need money in on-demand savings accounts to meet the unexpected. But trying to accumulate substantial sums that beat inflation that way is always tough. Only by careful long-term investment in shares (and property, as we see in chapter 19) is it likely that you will reach a sum that will give you a comfortable retirement. If you start in your 20s, and do nothing more than save the daily cost of a lunchtime sandwich and coffee, that is £1,200 a year. That is easily enough on average returns to build a fund of over £200,000 to retire on.

None of this is rocket science, just three common-sense principles: start early, make your money work hard for you, and leave it in peace to do its job.

CHAPTER 3.
Finance for Life

Introduction

A LOT OF BOOKS ON INVESTMENT CONCENTRATE ALMOST exclusively on fear of poverty in retirement as the motivation for saving, but in fact there are many other far less depressing reasons to get your money working. Once you have that habit of putting money away and getting it to multiply over a decade or more, you make the most of life's many opportunities. Not just the obvious sun-drenched Caribbean holidays or the gleaming red Ferrari, but subtler joys, like creating enough breathing space to let a partner give up a hated job or work part-time for a year; perhaps changing down a gear in your own career or taking an additional qualification. Planned long enough ahead, even the distant dreams become possible: buying the big country house in the Chilterns, a new life making goat's cheese in the Dordogne, or buying a home in an Andalucian olive grove.

Let's face it, if you spend every penny as soon as you get it, it isn't going to happen. But solid savings, started early and invested well, give you a freedom to live your life just the way you want. You are only limited by your imagination. This chapter will show you that:

- Saving is about setting yourself free.

- You can juggle the big expenses during your working life...

- ... but must plan for those when you have stopped working.

- You should embrace the idea of a long and active retirement...

- ... and learn, while young, how to provide for it.

One uniquely important decision

The good things in life are expensive, and the bills are never far away: a car, a deposit for a house, children, their school and university fees.

Sometimes we don't plan too carefully how we are going to afford them, because unconsciously we know we can manage somehow. We or our partners can press hard for that promotion, do a little moonlighting, or rack up overtime. We can scrimp and save at home, or miss out on a holiday. If all else fails, then the new car is smaller than we had hoped, or the private school less prestigious. So long as we still have working life ahead, we can juggle the bills and most of us seem to get by.

But there comes a time in life when everything depends on the quality of the decisions that were made earlier, sometimes decades earlier. When you are 75, perhaps unable to work, and the money you put by has run out, there is almost nothing you can do to put it right. If you made no pension provision, then whatever the state pension is, that's your lot. That is what makes planning for retirement a uniquely important decision, and that is why the rest of the chapter is devoted to it.

Ah yes, planning for retirement. This is the kind of phrase that pulls the keys out of the mental ignition for most 20-year-olds. For them the images are fixed: zip-up woolly slippers and incontinence pads, walking sticks and dentures. Someone's grandma, shivering alone in a dingy flat with a blanket over her knees watching *Coronation Street*.

The young cannot imagine life at 50, let alone 75. "I'm never going to be like that, no way," they say. "I'm not even going to think about it. Besides, I don't expect to live that long."

The best way to make that awful image of aged poverty into a reality is not to plan for retirement early enough. As shown in chapter 1, a 16-year-old can provide for retirement for the price of a pint of lager and a packet of crisps a day. Leave provision until you are 40 or 50 and we are talking about missing annual holidays, settling for a small second-hand car or forgetting private school for the kids. No wonder that by then many people cannot face the required sacrifices, and just hope for the best.

Today's reality is that those older people whose finances are in shape are doing pretty much everything the young are doing, whether it be going to the gym, lying on the beach, or walking holidays in the Himalayas. Increasingly healthy well into their 70s, today's older people have the greatest combination of leisure time and disposable income of any group. The pensioners, if you watch carefully, are the ones who are staying on at the skiing chalet for a second or third week while we, poor fools, have to fly home either because we don't have the money or because our boss needs us back at the office. Yes, and when that bearded man in leathers on the brand new Harley-Davidson Road King takes off his helmet … gasp! He's old enough to be a granddad!

Ripe old age

We in the western nations are living longer than ever before, and a greater proportion of that long life is likely to be a healthy one. Life expectancy in the UK for those born in 2012 is 79 years for a man and almost 83 for a woman, according to the Office of National Statistics.[3] If you were born in 1947, have made it unscathed through rationing, the 1950s' smogs, and the delightful excesses of the 1960s to reach 65 in

---

3   That is three more years since the first edition of this book came out in 2001.

2012, the view is even better. You can expect to live a further 21 years if you are a woman, and 18 if you are a man.[4] By 2035 there will be 110,000 British centenarians compared to 13,000 in 2010. Yet back in 1951 a 65-year-old would as often as not fail to reach their 70th birthday.

Longer life expectancy is a wonderful thing, so long as it is combined with quality of life in older age. However, there are other more dour individuals, namely economists, actuaries and demographers, who are extremely concerned. They point out that the biggest effect of an ageing population and generally low birth rates is the ballooning proportion of retired people relative to those of working age. In the UK that proportion increased from 17.6% in 1960 to 25% in 2011. Similar effects can be seen across developed nations.

Economists fret that those of working age face a double burden in supporting those who are not. "Disaster!" they warn. "Everybody is healthier and living longer." Clearly, despite the absence of world wars, asteroid impacts and plague, we will never run out of things to worry about.

The biggest and most obvious error is the crude pigeonholing of those under 65 as workers and those over that age as dependants. If health and mobility are reaching up into the 70s and 80s, why not employment too? The government has partially recognised that in its sliding scale of state pension entitlement thresholds, which get higher the later you are born. Even if the retirement age was lifted to 75 tomorrow (not something I'm advocating), the life expectancy of those retiring would still substantially exceed that of 1960s' 65-year-old retirees. The impact of increased participation in work would be powerful, because one worker extra is also one dependant fewer, thus affecting both sides of the workforce ratio.

I suspect the easiest adjustment would be to make retirement age a

---

4   Those who retire in 2014 have a better total life expectancy than those born in 2014 despite all the medical improvements available today because they already have 60–65 safe years under their belt. If we went back to, say, 1940 and measured life expectancy at birth we would have to include all those who didn't make it, which would cut the average expectancy enormously.

matter of personal preference more than government edict. Many older people delight in the companionship and challenge of work, either part-time or full-time, and because of improved health this is only going to increase in the future. We as a society will learn to be more open to the skills and experience they have.

Already thousands of grandparents use Skype to talk to younger relatives across the world. By 2030 those who were born in 1965 will be reaching 65. That generation spent its adult life firmly in the computer age. By then there will inevitably be a vastly expanded choice of work which can be done from home, using the computer and faster telecommunications. Perhaps the jump in self-employment showing up in official figures is the start of it.

Whether it be writing advertising copy, teaching an English literature course by video-link, or working for a 'virtual' call centre distributed across hundreds of homes, there is no reason why those in their late 60s and 70s cannot be part of the workforce. How much better than being left isolated and feeling dependent!

Future pensions

If we have learned anything from the global financial crisis, banking rescues and austerity of 2007 onwards, it is that even developed western economies can have trouble meeting their commitments to the population, and particularly to the retired. Do not assume the state will always be able to meet its promises. The current government has in place a 'triple lock' pledge on pensions, which ensures they grow each year in line with the higher of retail prices, average earnings or 2.5%. That is an enormous hostage to fortune, ratcheting up the proportion of national income eaten by pensions. It is unsustainable in the long term, even if the proportion of the elderly to those paying taxes stabilises.[5]

---

5   The theoretical arguments hold irrespective of what kind of pension provision is assumed. It is a truism that those who are not producing goods and services can only consume what

So if we cannot rely on the state pension, what can we rely on? The truth is that we must rely on ourselves. We must plan and work for our own retired future, just as we did for our education, employment and bringing up children. And just like all these things, if we put enough energy into it we might end up enjoying ourselves. There is a tremendous feeling of empowerment in controlling your own financial destiny.

How much will I need?

Anyone more than a few years from retirement is going to find it very difficult to work this out because of the number of variables:

- How healthy am I going to be?

- Will I be widowed?

- Will I be made redundant?

- Will I need to support aged relatives?

- How will the economy fare?

- Will there be changes to tax and benefits that affect me?

If you are young you will have absolutely no idea, but that isn't a problem. As we have seen, a modest amount put away every month from your early 20s should give you ample to cover most retirement contingencies. (Chapter 5 shows you how to choose a pension.) The decisions become a bit more challenging by middle age, when you have less time to put matters right.

those who are producing are willing not to consume. Economic theory contends that those who own private pensions based on financial assets such as shares or bonds will be squeezed by inflation caused by higher wages, while those dependent on state benefits will be squeezed by a wage earners' revolt over tax burdens. However, this theory does seem to accord the labour force more power than they have ever been able to exercise in practice.

CHAPTER 4.
The Pensions Minefield

Introduction

THIS CHAPTER DELVES INTO THE DETAILS OF THE THREE TYPES OF pension which are supposed to take us safely into retirement. They are:

1. **state pensions,** based on your national insurance (NI) record.

2. **occupational pensions,** provided by – or at least through – an employer.

3. **personal pensions**, provided from your own contributions.

Each of them has various sub-categories, and as with anything subject to government policies, can get rather complex.[6] Indeed, at the time of writing the government is due to publish more details about pension freedoms following the removal of the compulsion to buy an annuity. There is no need to plough through all the details, this is more of an à la carte chapter. Some readers may prefer to skip to chapter 5 for a

---

6   I have not attempted to replicate the level of detail found in the original 2001 edition, because so many up-to-date online resources are now available. Inevitably what is recorded here will also be overtaken by changes in legislation, some of which are still in train following the 2014 Budget.

quick overview of how to choose a pension, and then refer back to this chapter for a closer look at areas of interest. The pension and life insurance industry terms used here are explained in the glossary.

Pension savings versus non-pensions

There is a school of thought which sees pensions as being no better than other kinds of tax-protected saving. A company, personal or self-invested pension lets you put the contributions in untaxed (i.e. it not only credits the pension with your contribution from net pay but also adds back the income tax you paid). This means that £100 is invested for you if your contributions from net pay are £80 a month (adding back in basic rate tax). If you are a 40% taxpayer, you get £100 invested for each £60 contributed from net pay, but like any higher rate contribution, only the basic relief is added at source. The rest is adjusted through your tax return, up to an annual allowance of £40,000 (2014/15). Contributions beyond this can still be made but do not attract tax relief. A lifetime allowance of £1.25 million in pension contributions is also in force, but if this is an issue you are unlikely to need this book!

Most of those with an occupational pension get a contributory portion from their employer as well as that from their own toil, a unique advantage. The other side of the pensions coin is that all pensions are treated as taxable income in retirement, though you will have a higher personal allowance.

The usual comparison is with an individual savings account (ISA), which gives you no tax credit on contributions but gives you the eventual proceeds free of tax. Changes in the 2014 Budget have basically pooled the stocks and shares and savings elements of an ISA and dramatically increased the contribution limit. (There is more on using an ISA for investments in chapter 10.) An ISA remains a foundation stone for both savings and investments, and the ability to get your hands on the money quickly through an ISA makes them part of the middle tier of the savings pyramid covered in chapter 8. The same cannot be said for a pension, even in the new era of flexibility post-2014. An unexpected lump sum taken from a pension could easily push you into the 40% tax band. Better to take it from the ISA, then gradually refill the ISA from your regular pension withdrawals.

Don't forget the government

Ultimately, any government wants you to provide for your retirement. It isn't just the worry that a lot of poor and angry pensioners will start voting Monster Raving Loony to get rid of them (although voting intentions are never far from a government's mind). It is a question of public finances. Every penny you provide for your retirement is a penny the government won't have to find. Nothing is more tiresome for a government than finding that its social security budget gets blown every year because hundreds of thousands of people retire on the state basic pension alone, find they don't have enough to live on, then end up claiming benefits.

That is the motivation behind the workplace pension, introduced in 2012, which is run by employers to encourage employees to contribute towards their retirement. Whatever new schemes are brought in – and you can be sure they will change as frequently in the future as they have in the past – they will be formulated to encourage savings for retirement. So go with the flow, make a good pension a central plank in your savings strategy. And while you are at it, get an ISA too!

The state pension

The basic state pension, currently £113.10 a week (2014/15), was traditionally paid to women at 60 and men aged 65 or over. Since 2010 changes have begun to bring women's retirement age into line with men by 2020, and to increase the overall retirement age for both sexes, but this will not affect anyone born before 6 April 1950.

The payment is based on your own NI contributions, but is funded through taxation on those currently in work. It thus works in a wholly different way from other pensions which rely on the proceeds of investment.

It is very important to check your contributions record for the state pension. Those who do not have a full contributions record may receive only a partial pension. A year's work may not qualify if you failed to pay contributions for as little as four out of the 52 weeks. The self-employed, married women, those who changed jobs frequently, immigrants and those who have done a lot of casual work should be particularly careful to check their contributions record with their local benefits agency. Don't wait until you are approaching retirement! It is possible to buy back the last ten years' worth of any missed contributions, and it really makes sense to do so because the cost is recouped very quickly.

Married couples where one does not have a full contribution record may be able to claim a partial pension based on their partner's earnings. Normally it is a woman with a patchy NI record relying on her husband's pension once he retires. Same-sex couples in civil partnerships have the same rights as those who are married.

Pension credit is a means-tested benefit which tops up the income of those on basic state pensions. One element of it, savings credit, may be claimed by those who have savings; effectively a government nod to those who have attempted to put money away on their own accord.

Divorced or widowed

If you are divorced and not entitled to a full basic pension you may be able to use your former spouse's contribution record to boost your own pension up to the single person rate. A widow or widower who has reached pensionable age but does not qualify may also use their spouse's contribution record to qualify for the full basic pension.

Carers

Home responsibilities protection (HRP) started in 1978 and ended in 2010, when it was replaced by NI credits. Both schemes are designed to protect the state pension rights of anyone who has cared for a child or a sick or disabled person for a whole tax year or more. There are some fairly stringent conditions. If you have ever missed working through bringing up a child, or looking after a relative, make sure your NI record reflects the credits to which you are entitled. Don't wait until retirement looms!

Deferring your pension: worth considering

On retirement, you can choose to defer your state pension for up to five years, and will get 10.4% more for each year that you do so. You can also take this as a lump sum with an added interest bonus for each year deferred. Given current life expectancy at retirement this could be a winner for those who want to carry on working or have alternative sources of income.

The additional state pension

Previously known as the state second pension, the additional state pension is an earnings-related pension that replaced the state earnings-related pension scheme (SERPS) in 2002. Essentially it is designed to bolster the pension of those who are in employment but only earning between £5,772 and £15,100 (2014/15). Accrual rates vary, dependent upon earnings in different bands.

Occupational pensions

Occupational pensions are the pensions that the majority of people have, and if you intend to remain with the same employer for a substantial length of time it has always made sense to have one (unless that employer's name was Robert Maxwell, which meant it ended up supporting his lifestyle rather than yours).

If you work for the NHS or a local authority, your pension might be one of the few real advantages you have over your friends working in the private sector.

If you just look at your pay slips and what you get when you retire, all occupational schemes seem to work the same way. They take a contribution from you and a contribution from your employer while you are employed, and give you a monthly sum when you retire. All give you the chance to take a lump sum of up to a quarter of the fund tax-free at retirement. The rest always used to have to go into a special fund called an annuity from which the pension was paid when you retire. All that changed with the 2014 Budget, which has thrown out the hated annuity. What might replace it we will deal with later.

Although at first glance most occupational schemes look the same, there are important differences. A few parts of the public sector, such as the police, use a pension mechanism identical to that of a state pension, where current employees fund current retirees. Most others, and all employers in the private sector, use stock-market-related investment funds that build up over time. Until a decade ago most occupational schemes used a defined benefits approach, sometimes called final salary schemes.

Final salary schemes

The day you start paying into a defined benefits fund, you know what proportion of your final salary you will receive on retirement. It might be something like one-sixtieth of your final salary for each year of service. This gives you half your final salary if you leave after 30 years, but only one-sixth if you serve only ten years. (See section on job changers.)

This level of benefit is guaranteed by the pension fund, whether the stock market performs well or badly, and even if all the scheme's pensioners live to be 100. This guarantee gives employees peace of mind, but is increasingly giving employers sleepless nights, because they are taking all the investment risk. They are required to bail out the fund if it can't maintain the required benefits or can keep the extra if there is more in the pension pot than required by the benefits. They were happy with that in the 1980s when investment performance was ripping along and there were plenty of 'fund holidays' when companies stopped making contributions to an already brimming pensions pot. But now with pensioners living longer, very low interest rates, and a less-exuberant investment climate, occupational fund deficits are much more likely than a surplus.[7]

Money purchase schemes

This has led to the growth of defined contribution schemes (also called money purchase), in which the employee in effect takes the investment risk. They are the vast majority of schemes, particularly for new employees. While they do not necessarily perform worse than final salary schemes, they may well come with lower employer contributions and a great deal more complexity and anxiety for the employee. If you start work for an employer which has a defined contribution scheme you will be free to decide how much of your pay you want to put into your pension, but the employer can define its contributions too. Some employers match your contributions pound for pound, while others may pay only 10% of what you contribute.

Then there are the choices you have to make. There may be a bewildering variety of different funds on offer for you to choose from as you build up a portfolio to suit your risk profile, and most people will need advice. There are default options for those

---

7   If your employer has a chronically underfunded pension, and is in difficulties itself, you may not automatically get your pension in full. Though the government has a safety-net scheme, the Pension Protection Fund, it is as well to be aware in advance where problems might occur.

who can't face the choices, but they are not always the best value or most suitable. Pensions are like abattoirs – we know we need them, but would rather pay extra not to get involved in the gory details. Unfortunately, problems in the system are forcing us to peek through the door at the grim workings within.

The upshot of all this is that if you are starting work at a new employer and are offered a pension there is a great deal more to consider than there used to be. Whether we want to or not, we are being forced to take more responsibility for our financial future – right down to assessing the performance of the investment engine within.

Additional voluntary contributions (AVCs)

Additional voluntary contributions are a kind of turbocharger for your occupational pension. When they are run by an employer, they can be a very effective way of turning a good occupational scheme into an even better one for those who feel that they may not have enough to live comfortably at retirement. However, there is a class of AVCs called FSAVCs (freestanding additional voluntary contributions) which have a rather less-attractive pedigree. They are supplied independently of your employer, and may be expensive in some cases. Mis-selling of FSAVCs is just one of the many scandals to dog the pension industry.

Workplace pension

The workplace pension, which replaced the stakeholder pension as a workplace scheme in 2012, is the government's safety net for employees, an attempt to build in the savings habit amongst the many low-paid and part-time employees who often don't get round to building a pension. From 2015 every employer, even the smallest, must enrol any UK employee who is at least 22 and earns at least £10,000 a year. A typical contribution might be £80 per month; £40 from the employee, £30 from the employer and £10 from the government. The principle is exactly the same as employer-sponsored schemes, but there are minimum total contribution levels of 2% of your qualifying income, rising to 8% by 2018.

The criticisms of the workplace pension, like its predecessor and like many other pension vehicles, are really over the cost and efficiency of the investment engine that produces the return. Fees from investment and insurance companies that provide the product, the minimum size of workplace schemes, and the inefficiency of dealing with tiny contributions all cast some doubt on how effective a weapon these will turn out to be in helping employees provide effectively for their own old age. However, those who are tempted to opt out should consider that an employer contribution is very valuable, and should not lightly be discarded.

Things have improved since the days of the personal pension, the government's first stab at pension portability. Providers are not allowed to charge you for transferring in or out of the scheme, or if you stop paying contributions for a while. However, they are still allowed to recoup other costs of running the fund, like the 0.5% stamp duty paid on their share transactions, or the cost of sharing a pension if a couple divorces. Services such as pension advice or life-assurance cover would be on top of the legal minimum.

Stakeholder pensions

While superseded as a workplace pension, stakeholder pensions still exist as a standalone personal pension. They have annual charge limits of 1.5%, which isn't very cheap, but this must fall to 1% after ten years.[8] The big remaining advantage is their flexibility, which allows those not in employment to use investment proceeds in a highly tax-efficient way.

A stakeholder pension allows you to provide a pension for anyone you choose, so the better off can provide for a non-working spouse,

---

8   Those doubting that 1.5% is a lot of money should glance back again at the section on costs and performance in chapter 2.

a child or a grandchild and get relief at the standard rate, or for themselves at the higher rate. There is a £3,600 annual limit on contributions for those who are not working, which for a standard-rate taxpayer costs only £2,800 from net income. For a 40% taxpayer, the cost is just £2,180.

Pay that £3,600 limit into a child's stakeholder annually from birth to the age of 18, then leave it alone and by retirement the little tyke will be worth a cool half million, assuming investment returns of only a miserly 4%.

Personal pensions

Personal pensions are essentially money purchase schemes, with returns tied to how much you contribute and returns on the stock market. Their heyday was in the 1990s, and many people still have them, though they have been superseded by the workplace pension for new employees. They were a first legislative stab at providing a pension to give a degree of flexibility for those who changed employers, were made redundant, took time out of work or became carers. They were often inefficient, with high annual charges, penalties for changing contribution levels and poor transfer values. Basically, every change you made cost you money.

We will cover management charges and performance in depth when we look at active management, but suffice it to say that even small management charges nibble away quite a lot of your stash in the long run, and the universal bragging by these funds of superior (i.e. market-beating) performance is as illusory as the manager of any Premier League football club vowing never to let his team drop into the bottom half of the table. One more thing to remember. Who do you think is paying for all these bragging advertisements? That's right – you are.

High initial charges (also called front-end loading) and annual management charges have one thing in common, beyond making financial salesmen very happy, and that is that they ride roughshod over two of the three key rules of multiplying your money. These rules are **start early** and **small differences in return matter**. The initial commission means you are actually starting up your investment vehicle a year and a half later than you imagined, while the annual charge means you will be doing the entire trip with the handbrake on.

Self-invested personal pensions (SIPPs)

A self-invested personal pension is a pension where you select the investments which go into your retirement fund. Available since the 1980s, they have in recent years become the vehicle of choice for those with a little investment self-confidence and an eye for saving fees. SIPPs are offered by the same kinds of stockbrokers who offer ISAs. The charges vary hugely, sometimes depending on the size of your portfolio, and in most cases involve a flat annual fee and a dealing charge for each purchase of a fund or other security. The best of them offer pretty comprehensive and competitively priced execution-only services for a wide variety of markets both here and abroad.

What happens on retirement?

It's all very well pouring money into a pension plan, but how you turn that into accessible income in retirement is absolutely vital. Since the Budget of 2014, which swept away the requirement to buy an annuity, pensioners now have a great deal more freedom over how they spend their retirement money. Instead of just being able to take 25% out as a lump sum, from April 2015 they are able to take it all out, though subject to tax. That should be fantastic news, particularly getting rid of the hated annuity, but it still presents some complex choices to those who are about to retire.

The full implications of this momentous change have yet to be seen, and no doubt the insurance and pensions industry is in the process of dreaming up new products to offer, but it is still possible to draw broad conclusions. First of all, though, we need to look at the annuity – not least because some pensioners are stuck with one, and in some cases it will still make sense to have one.

Annuities

A basic annuity is a chunk of capital which is largely invested in government bonds and property. The income is fixed at purchase and is used to pay you a monthly sum until death. On your death, the remaining capital is retained by the provider company. How much you get depends on how long you are expected to live, and whether you opt for a more complex annuity which might include an annual inflation-linked increase and a widow's benefit. Those with health problems might benefit from a higher annuity rate, known as 'impaired life', because they are expected to die more quickly than the average.

However, the general trend in recent years has been miserable for pensioners. The average 65-year-old male pensioner with a £100,000 pension pot will get less than £5,000 a year now. That is less than half the £11,380 he would have got in 1995, according to *Moneyfacts*. That isn't quite the tumble in living standards that it seems, however, as inflation is lower now than the 3.5% it was then, so the purchasing power of the fixed payment would be maintained for longer. Still, it is certainly a headline shock.

Until March 2014, almost everybody who contributed to a money-purchase pension scheme needed, at some point in retirement, to buy an annuity. Those with final salary schemes were the main exception.

Drawdown

The other option that already existed before the 2014 Budget was drawdown, which allows you to take income from your pension pot while it remains invested. You can choose how much pension you want to be paid each year within certain limits. There are two forms of drawdown, capped and flexible.

Capped drawdown pension

With a capped drawdown pension there's a maximum amount you can draw each year but no minimum amount. This annual limit is related to the size of the pot, and life expectancy calculation. Exceeding the annual limit is possible, but incurs a hefty tax charge. Drawdown has the tremendous advantage compared to an annuity of allowing you access to the capital as well as the income of your pot. The downside is that these huge freedoms could lead to mistakes, the most obvious one being running out of money. It is worth bearing in mind that because of the actuarial reviews of drawdown limits it is possible for the maximum allowed withdrawal to fall.

Flexible drawdown pension

To qualify for flexible drawdown you must already be getting a pension of at least £12,000 each year (it was £20,000 before the 2014 Budget) from other 'secure pensions' such as the state pension, most lifetime annuities and pensions paid from defined benefits schemes. With flexible drawdown there's no limit to the amount you can draw from your pension scheme in any year, because the government reckons that your other income will see you through if you make a mistake. You can either leave it all in the scheme, or take part or all of it, though you will be taxed at your marginal rate.

But even if you don't meet the minimum secure pension threshold, you may be able to take your whole pension fund as a lump sum if you have a small pension pot. The 2014 Budget increased the definition of a small pot from £18,000 to £30,000. This is interesting because 'small' in this instance is actually average. About half of men, and many more women, have a pension pot worth less than this at retirement. So in one fell swoop the chancellor has taken around half the working population out of the complexity of drawdown.

Watch out for exit charges

The new pension freedoms, which come into force in April 2015, may come with a sting in the tail. Existing schemes are still in force, and pension providers are not forced to offer those within them the same freedoms that new policyholders have. Those planning to switch pensions may find that substantial exit charges will be levied. At the time of writing, ministers are being lobbied by consumer groups to take action to ensure that long-suffering pensioners are not hit again when they leave such schemes. In the meantime it seems likely that pension schemes are going to be given more freedom to make one-off payments to pensioners.

Women and retirement

First the good news: women, as we know, live longer than men – four years on average, although the gap is closing. For now, women can still retire earlier than men. That means women have up to nine additional years when they would expect to be paid a pension compared with men. To put it another way, women need to save more than men to retire on the same income. With many people likely to avoid annuities and choose some form of drawdown, this makes the situation more acute.

According to Prudential, women expect to retire on just £12,000 a year, while men anticipate £18,000. Married women in the past have often relied on being provided for by their husband and the husband's pension, but often did not realise that they may survive a husband, especially one who had a manual occupation, not by one or two years, but by a decade or more. Although that gap has closed in recent years, the fact remains that women need to be even more careful than men about providing for retirement, because they are likely to experience much more of it. Moreover, with divorce rates climbing among older couples, women of later years need to be more pro-active about ensuring they provide for themselves in retirement.

The same advice prevails for women's pension provision as for every other form of saving. Start early, get the best rate of return you can, and keep contributing. Don't rely on the state pension or the means-tested safety nets. Check your NI contributions early, and be prepared to buy back missing contributions. You will find that they pay for themselves very quickly.

Pension scandals

Throughout the financial services industry for the last 50 years there has been one mis-selling scandal after another. Commission-driven salesmen offering products to poorly educated consumers that were expensive, inadequate, unsuitable and downright dangerous. Payment protection insurance (PPI), interest-only mortgages, contracting out of state-earnings-related pensions; the list is almost endless. The first mis-sold product, the endowment policy, was a perfect example of a product suitable for almost nobody. The tale of Equitable Life perhaps exemplified what could go wrong.

Equitable Life, which still exists but no longer sells products, was a mutually owned life-insurance company, with a very large market share in with-profits policies. These policies shared a portion of the funds' investment success with policyholders. All right and proper in a mutually owned company, after all. From the 1950s through to the 1980s it sold with-profits policies, with guaranteed annuity rate options attached. This meant that it had promised policyholders that they could opt on retirement for an annuity guaranteeing a certain annual income for life based on the size of the pension contributions they were paying. When those promises were made, they were way below the rates Equitable actually paid, and the actuaries who estimated life expectancies and required funding thought the guarantees, though a useful marketing tool for the nervous policyholder, would never be called on.

But the trouble with pensions is that you are making a promise in 1950 or 1970 and expecting to cover all eventualities 30, 40 or even 50 years later. It is this broader truth that makes this tale worth recounting in detail. Ironically, Equitable managed to corner a lot of business over this period because its charges were relatively low, and it was paying out most of what it earned to investors in annual and terminal bonuses, and not squirrelling away huge chunks of investors' cash for itself. There would have been nothing to stop it doing this. Most other life insurers did.

Lack of transparency

The amazing thing is that policyholders so trusted Equitable Life and the other life insurers in spite of a lack of concrete evidence of how the underlying funds were performing. The funds were smoothed, so that in good investment years part of the returns made in shares, governments bonds and property were held back to build up a financial reserve and in bad years that reserve was drawn on to fund annuity commitments and bonuses. Policyholders were never told, and certainly would not be expected to understand if they were told, how the investment returns were calculated.

The actuaries were answerable to no one, and where with-profits policies still exist, that remains the case. Unlike unit trusts or investment trusts, where investors can at least see how many units or shares they own, with-profits was an alchemist's factory, in which the small amounts of base metal delivered by policyholders at the gates were turned as if by magic into retirement gold a few decades hence.

The investment returns in the market held up over the years, but the death rate among those who held annuities began to decline. Then, to make matters worse, the fall in the average level of interest rates during the 1980s and 1990s began to cut into the returns earned on gilt-edged securities, the cornerstone of annuity funding. So Equitable Life, like other life insurers, began to cut annuity rates. By late 1993 annuity rates fell below those offered in the guarantee options. However, in an act of astonishing arrogance, the insurer said it would cut the final bonuses of those choosing the guaranteed annuity, making the guarantee worthless. Equitable Life's actuaries, paid to consider all probabilities, presumably didn't see any chance the courts might uphold the guarantees, and indeed they won cases brought by policyholders until the matter went to the House of Lords in the summer of 2000, seven years later. They then lost, but that wasn't the end of it because the money just wasn't there. In the end investors of all stripes lost a huge proportion of their pensions, and Equitable Life's operating businesses were sold. The moral of the tale is: never take a guarantee at face value.

Conclusion

The subject of pensions is a maze and probably always will be. Year after year, surveys show that those who will need extra resources above those provided by the state pension are those least likely to put plans in place to provide them. The less-well-paid, part-timers, those who change jobs frequently or work casually, women, those from ethnic minorities, all tend to have below-average take-up rates for occupational pension schemes or pension products. In the past, various mis-selling episodes, scandalous charging structures and lack of clear information have all combined to add one extra obstacle to those already reluctant to provide for their future. The main challenges remaining are, as always, to start early enough and to contribute enough. While no one can know exactly how much they will need ten, 20 or 30 years hence, the sensible decision is always 'as much as you comfortably can'. And if by some chance you reach that retirement age and find it is more than you need, you can always have fun like a 16-year old: spend it!

CHAPTER 5.
The Briefest Possible Guide to Choosing a Pension

Introduction

THIS IS THE SHORTEST POSSIBLE GUIDE TO CHOOSING A PENSION. Definitions and explanations can be found in chapter 4 and in the glossary. The answers are broad-brush, because individual circumstances vary. Don't assume this is all the information you will need. The Pensions Advisory Service offers free advice, or an independent financial advisor can take a more detailed look at your circumstances, usually for a fee. The government set aside £20m in its 2014 pension legislation to help those at retirement get independent advice. Do make sure you get it! But actually, the most important decisions are those made decades earlier.

Occupational pensions should be your first choice so long as your employer makes a contribution. The most dependable of these are defined benefit schemes (which tell you what proportion of final pay you will receive). If the amount contributed seems small, or you are late starting, consider additional voluntary contributions (AVCs) so long as the scheme is run by your employer. For most people, it will be a money purchase scheme. Though some of these have high embedded charges, the employer contribution should more than offset them. Workplace pensions will be the default for all where an employer hasn't hitherto offered a pension.

For those with just a little investment self-confidence, a self-invested personal pension with an array of low-cost stock market trackers can be a low-maintenance, cheap and effective way of meeting your long-term retirement objectives.

Pension savings vs benefits

Bear in mind that if your circumstances really are limited, and you are starting late, it may not be worth trying to create significant pension savings. You may lose almost as much in benefit on retirement as you gain in income. Pension credit guarantees that no one will end up with less than £148.35 per week (2014/15) to live on. The uprating of these kind of benefits has since 2010 been tied into a generous (and ultimately unsustainable) uprating called the triple-lock, where state pension benefits rise by the highest of inflation, average earnings or 2.5% each year. That is a recipe for an ever-expanding share of national income to be allocated to an ever-expanding retired demographic, funded by those in work. I'm frankly surprised it has lasted even this long. Certainly, we should expect it to be made less generous within a decade.

Change is the one constant: investment returns, inflation, your income and circumstances, and your employer will probably change frequently during a working lifetime. Tax rules, relief and benefit levels almost always change with each new chancellor of the exchequer. Keep an eye on your pension arrangements, and err on the side of generosity in your contributions.

Pensions common sense

- Don't put off a decision – start early and save yourself money.

- Shop around. Never sign for anything on the spot.

- Find out what you are getting. Read the small print.

- Will your pension be invested in the stock market? Ask!

- Look at charges. Even a charge of 1% a year will consume a quarter of all the money you save in a 25-year policy.

- Think about job change and what effect this will have on the pension.

- Once you have signed up, you still have several days to change your mind, without cost. It isn't too late to do some last-minute shopping around!

Finally, remember that retirement is intended to be fun. This is why you worked for all those years, right? Make sure you have enough put by to relax and use that leisure time to its fullest extent.

CHAPTER 6.
Finding the Money to Multiply

"Annual income twenty pounds, annual expenditure nineteen and six, result happiness. Annual income twenty pounds, annual expenditure twenty pound and six, result misery."

Mr Micawber, in *David Copperfield* by Charles Dickens

Introduction

BEFORE YOU BEGIN MULTIPLYING ANY MONEY YOU HAVE GOT TO find some money in the first place. The big commitments of a mortgage, children, bills, and the family car (or two) seem to eat up whatever is earned and there is often month left at the end of the money instead of the other way around. If you are the sort of person who steams off unfranked stamps or takes the light bulbs with you when you move house, then you probably don't need this chapter. But if you keep £10,000 in a current account, or buy a health-club membership and never go, well, you might find this useful. Let's face it, we all squander some money, but sometimes it just seems too much trouble to do anything about it.

Some people are good at discovering where the money goes, while others are not. Most of us fall somewhere in the middle, with a reasonable feel for the big regular bills such as mortgage and council tax, but a much hazier idea how much we spend on the irregular and variable items such as holidays and meals out, and those seemingly small outlays like mobile phone bills, a punt on the lottery, and that daily avocado and bacon baguette from the sandwich shop across from the office.

When I decided to leave paid employment and become a freelance writer I gritted my teeth, sat down and worked out all my outgoings to see how much I would need to make. The biggest revelations were all in the categories I had assumed were insignificant. One was that I spent more on newspapers than I did on heating my home, and the second was that the large coffee I had just started getting daily from one of those trendy cafés would, if I kept the habit up, cost me almost as much a year as council tax. So, when I decided to pare back to the essentials, it was surprising how easily it was done.

A financial check-up

It isn't a bad idea to plan out your spending and income once a year, whether you are having trouble making ends meet or not. It becomes essential if you are going through a major change in life: when moving in with a partner, divorcing, considering moving home or job, or if you have been recently widowed. Like many things in life the hardest part is thinking about doing it. Once you get on with it you discover how easy most of it is.

As with many large tasks, it is easiest divided up into pieces. Start small, perhaps reconciling your cash withdrawals with receipts, and let it flow from there. Get yourself a new concertina file, clearly label each section and then get a good-sized wastepaper bin. For every piece of important paper that needs filing, there are probably two pieces that will end up in the bin.

Once you have added up how much you spend in an average month (and had a double whisky to recover from the shock) you can do the easier bit, which is working out your income. In many cases this just requires one piece of paper, your annual P60 generated by your employer. The self-employed have a more complex job, but one required at least once a year anyway. If you are retired or disabled this might be mainly benefits or allowances, and you might be all too well aware of your income constraints. In any case don't forget to add in the interest from any savings you may have, making a mental note of what return you are getting on your money. Couples should make it a joint exercise, first because like decoration or weeding the garden it can make a solitary chore into something less onerous, but secondly because in any joint household the exercise isn't going to get you very far unless your spouse or partner is doing their bit.

Once you have gone to the trouble of assessing your income and outgoings, you might as well catalogue your assets and liabilities. An asset would be your home, for example, and a liability the loan you took out to buy it. If this was all you possessed, your net worth would be the current value of the house minus the size of the loan. Add up all the loans you have to repay on one side of a piece of paper or spreadsheet and the current value (as if you had to sell tomorrow) of the car, furniture and washing machine on the other. Don't forget your pension! Assets are not just the things that can be dragged down to a car-boot sale and sold.

This is also the time to seek out your forgotten assets. Grandma's jewellery, which was last valued in 1963 and now sits forgotten in a drawer; that collection of 1951 *Champion* comics on top of the wardrobe. Climb into the loft for a peek at that old chest of Aunt Elsie's, which she once mentioned had pre-war share certificates in. Take a shrewd look at that battered table you store crankcase halves on in the garage – is that antique French polish underneath the oil and grease? Once you take the time to dig around it is amazing what you can find. Lost keys, combs, receipts, that bag of brass cogs which was once your mother's chiming Swiss clock and which you took to pieces to clean in 1973 then couldn't work out how to put back together. Anyone who needs further inspiration only need watch *Antiques Roadshow* to get the saliva positively gushing.

There are also hidden liabilities, things which might happen and you might need to pay for: elderly relatives living in council housing who may soon need nursing home care, the rusting car that will soon have to be replaced, the flat bitumen roof on the garage which is beginning to leak. Finally, you think you know everything. You know how much comes into the house every month, and how much goes out, how big your debts are, and how much you own. Even the antique teapot on the sideboard has been counted.

Is there anything you have forgotten?

Yes. Yourself.

Putting a price on your head

This isn't the Wild West and slavery is gone, so why are we putting a price on our heads? The point is that what we have looked at so far are *static* finances, a kind of snapshot of what comes in and what goes out of the household. But finances change over the years, very much according to how we change. The value of the breadwinners in a household is the most important part of that. You might be amazed how much you are worth. A lifetime's income for many people starting work today at the age of 20 could be well over £2m. If you doubt me, look back, instead of into the future. We see that those who began work in the early 1950s typically earned £2–3 a week, perhaps £100–150 a year. In the mid-1990s they retired with annual salaries which could be £20,000–50,000. If you had told them in 1952 that they would eventually be earning 200 or even

500 times what they were paid in their first year of work, their eyes would have popped out on stalks.[9]

Naturally, a 1950s' pound, which could buy most of a week's groceries, is not the same as a 2014 pound which can't get you a serving of bread in many restaurants. But even after inflation, economic growth has meant that a lifetime's income, on average, is not just a substantial amount of money, but a much larger amount than would have been predicted. Until 2008, the promise that each generation would be richer than the last in real terms has on average held true. Even now, it is not possible to say that it will never be true again.

"So what?" you might say. "A lifetime's spending is pretty gigantic too." Of course, this is true. There are not just the things we have always paid for, such as heat and light and food, but now the essential car (or two), and televisions, which have gone from being a rarity in 1960 to one per home in 1970 and now, sometimes, one per room. Whole categories of new things to buy, such as smartphones (for the kids too) and health-club memberships, have arrived, while other kinds of spending once reserved for a few, including private schools, private health insurance, and domestic cleaning services, are enjoyed by many.

The point is that the bigger those two flows, income and expenditure, the more scope you have to make a difference. If you live in rural India and your only income is from firewood sold by the roadside and your only expenditure is the daily chapati you buy with the proceeds, then you don't have a lot of scope to create savings. But if you have been educated, acquired saleable skills, and developed self-confidence, then you have already turned yourself into a money machine that should increase in value throughout your life. Saving is not just about trimming spending, it is also about boosting income.

---

9   One way is to think of yourself as an investment and your annual salary as the interest you earn on your human capital. Using a typical mortgage interest rate of say 3.5%, someone with a £20,000 a year salary would be 'worth' £571,000.

Protecting your income

Anything that stands between you and your income can be a worry. Often we only worry about sickness or disability when we take out a mortgage, but there are a great many other bills to pay too. While we associate sickness or disability with 19th-century factory conditions, it is not so much physical injury as debilitating stress or psychological problems that we are now likely to encounter. Statistically, women are more likely than men to leave work because of sickness.

Of course, many people thought they were protecting against this with the many payment protection insurance schemes which in the last decade were forced upon those taking out mortgages or other loans. Now they have discovered that most of these policies were unsuitable if not unusable. The more than £10 billion of PPI compensation paid by banks to consumers is probably the biggest single injection of cash into the budgets of those of low-to-average income in recent years. The worst aspect of this is probably the tarnishing of the idea that you should insure against catastrophic loss of income. While it was never right for everyone, there are many people in well-paid, high-risk or high-stress jobs for whom such coverage is still a very good idea indeed.

The saving habit

The best saving habits start young. Some children learn to save their pocket money, accumulating it for a treat. It gives an understanding of the value of money and keeps at bay the urge for immediate gratification, the mortal enemy of money multiplication. Decades ago parents often used to put away a few shillings a week into an insurance policy which would come to maturity when the child reached 18 or 21. Even at the lowly rates of return then prevailing on such policies, it could often end up a tidy sum.

It is the habit and the idea that are crucial here. In a sense, it doesn't matter that the initial amounts saved are small, so long as they are regular. Better the £10 a month, rain or shine, than an irregular £100 when you remember to do it. The least painful way to save, in fact the least painful way to part with any money, is before you see it. This is particularly easy now almost all salaries are paid directly into a bank. So when you set up standing orders or direct debits for gas or electricity, that is the time to set up a payment to a savings account. It is amazing how you don't miss the money that way. If instead you wait until the end of the month to write a cheque into a savings account, you may have nothing left.

Love and money

Thinking the unthinkable is a vital last line of defence in both finance and relationships. Tens of thousands of people every year are left in dire financial straits when relationships disintegrate. Breaking up, particularly when children are involved, is extremely expensive, quite apart from the legal fees: two homes and households instead of one, childcare fees, endless driving to visit children, the treats inspired by guilt. This is bad enough for amicable break-ups, but real suffering can come from antagonistic partings. In these cases it is often the woman who finds herself in penury. Perhaps it is because nothing mentions her name: not the deeds to the house, not the savings accounts, not the car.

Divorce pitches some women of middle age into handling finances or paying bills for the first time, and the hardest time to learn how to handle money is when there isn't any.

When a clean-break divorce occurs, it is almost always the woman who receives a lump-sum settlement. For those unused to dealing with money this brings huge responsibilities and temptations. While the sum may appear huge in some cases, it has to cover unknown contingencies. Not only might it be hard to recognise when a house roof or car gearbox needs repair, but who to approach about fixing it and what is a reasonable price to pay can be worrying too.

Tying up the money, even into a good investment, may be unwise for those who have yet to get the hang of being mistress of their own finances. While some men are financially crushed by the terms of divorce settlements, women are more often left struggling because a partner fails to abide by the terms. The early months of a break-up, when shock and anger are at their greatest, can be particularly difficult. A partner who hasn't worked may be forced back into employment, often after a long gap, and may have trouble finding cash for day-to-day needs. Debt incurred at such times can take years to clear. While there is no way to avoid this completely, a mental checklist might stop you being caught unawares.

- Do you know how much your partner earns?

- Do you look after your personal finances?

- Is the house in joint names?

- Do you have a bank or savings account that is just in your own name and could not be emptied by a partner?

- Are there joint debts, such as credit cards and loans, as well as the mortgage, that you alone may have to shoulder if you remain in the house?[10]

Couples starting out should consider a prenuptial agreement, unromantic as it is, on who should get what if they break up. It is a far easier, cheaper, and quicker thing to decide in love than in hate. That applies to gay couples too, who are now thankfully on an almost equal legal footing with straight couples. If one partner handles all the household finances it is not doing the other one any favours, any more than a couple of whom only one knows how to drive. If you know nothing about how much money comes in or

---

10   Joint loans or cards often need both signatures for cancellation. If you are being pressed for debts run up by a partner, it is imperative to seek help quickly. Notify your bank and speak to your local Citizens Advice Bureau.

goes out of the household you may be storing up trouble for yourself. Secrecy about finances between couples can be a bad sign.

Saving for a rainy day

For the purposes of multiplying your money, saving modestly when young beats big savings in middle age. The irony is that saving often only comes easily to us late in life, when time is no longer on money's side. Once we have examined our finances, some of the easiest problems are quickly resolved: the magazines we order but never read, the utility bills which would be cheaper on direct debit, that exercise bike we never use, the special-occasion outfits that were worn once and then forgotten.

But for most of us there is a more complex knot: the mortgage, the bank accounts, and credit cards. So much gets poured in, we feel we must be able to save money here, but how? That is what we will tackle in the next two chapters.

CHAPTER 7.

Turning the Tables on Debt

Introduction

O NE OF THE OBVIOUS WAYS TO SAVE MONEY IS BY TACKLING debt. Debt has its uses, and there are many important things in life few of us could do without it, like buying a home or going to university. But no finance issue tangles up people as thoroughly as debt, and none ruins more lives.

Uncontrolled debt is a monster and it can consume everything you have. As Darth Vader might have said, it is the 'dark side' of compound interest. Even a small loan taken at 20–30% a year, the kind of rates that credit cards or finance companies frequently charge, can become too big to handle in a year or two if regular payments are not met in full (see Figure 7.1).

In addition to interest payments, there are often other charges; for example, credit cards often impose a hefty charge on those who do not pay off a minimum balance.

There are three major rules to tackling debt:

1. Don't delay – money mounts up.

2. Rates matter – more than you might think.

3. Know the difference between good debt and bad debt.

The first two rules are familiar because they are based on the same facts that apply to multiplying your money. The last is different and helps us judge *where* it is worthwhile taking on debt. Before we leave points 1 and 2, it is worth examining just how much trouble we can get into if we let debts mount up. In Figure 7.1, the shallower series is a £70,000 loan, charged at 7.5% – perhaps a very bad case of mortgage arrears – while the steep series is £7,000 run up on a credit card at 21.5%. The latter rate is three times the former, and in 20 years would multiply the debt 40-fold.

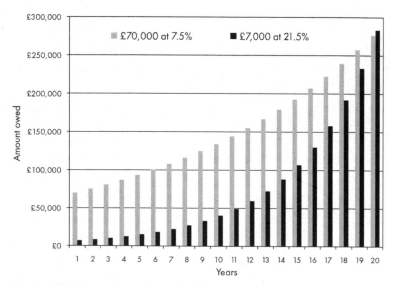

Figure 7.1. Comparison of unpaid debts over 20 years

Good debt and bad debt

These days we are constantly urged to get into debt, whether it be by banks offering us 'low-cost' loans because we have been good customers for years, an electrical retailer trying to get us to pay by instalments for a new TV, or the credit card firm that – noticing we always pay off the monthly balance – ups our credit limit to tempt us to overspend. So how do we work out when to take on fresh debt and when to refuse?

The crucial issue, just as important as the interest rate, is what you take out the loan to buy. Obvious extremes illustrate the principle. Not many people would be daft enough to take a loan to gamble on the horses even if the interest rate were only 5%, but few would quarrel with taking an overdraft at 10% to cover the costs of studying for a professional qualification which would lead to a big increase in salary. Backing your favourite horse in the St. Leger may give you plenty to pay off your loan if it wins, but if it does not you are clearly worse off than by not taking the loan. By contrast, the return on your qualification is a racing certainty (although you should be sure you can pass the exams!) and after the loan is paid off you will continue to reap the benefit of the extra salary. So a debt is good when it offers us some kind of return for the extra we are paying in interest, and bad when it does not. Here are three classic examples.

1. Car finance

Roughly three quarters of car sales are funded by credit, but it is one of the ultimate 'bad' debts. Getting a loan to buy a car is pretty much akin to taking out a mortgage on an ice cube. The underlying value of what we are getting just melts away. If we need a car and don't have the cash, we may not be able to do too much about it, but there is no doubt that knowing what it really costs might cool the zeal for that brand new Alfa Romeo or BMW and turn us toward an older model or something less flashy.

The real bugbear here is depreciation, which saps the resale value. That depreciation is in itself one of the reasons that the interest rate on a loan to purchase a car is so high – unlike a mortgage, the asset behind the loan will not cover your debt if you default. In short, the lender is taking more of a risk, and you are paying extra for that.

Say you buy a new Ford Focus 1.6 litre estate for £19,250 today. In four years, according to the *WhatCar* depreciation index, it will be worth £6,500. If you had financed that with a car loan, based on an average credit score and a 14.7% APR (quoted to me by CarLoans4U in August 2014) you would have paid £24,900 for it. Four years of driving that vehicle has cost you £18,400 – and that's before you put a drop of petrol in it! A home to use as loan security and haggling over the price of the car would all improve matters, but the real cost of debt-financed motoring is still a troubling one.

2. Student loans

Until a decade ago there would have been no doubt that student loans were a good debt, because they financed a real and reliable increase in lifetime earnings. Now, however, we cannot be so sure. That isn't just because of the soaring cost of education. More worryingly, there is a growing body of evidence that the earnings uplift from certain kinds of degrees isn't always enough to repay the debt, at least three years' lost income and to provide a positive lifetime return. A recent study[11] showed that while doctors and dentists made massive returns on their investment, men who studied art and design might have been better off just getting A-levels and getting into the industry three years earlier.

There is much uncertainty here, particularly around what would be the right rate to discount future earnings versus today's costs, but it is certainly worth taking a deeper look considering that six months

---

11   London School of Economics 2014, commissioned by the Department for Business.

after graduation, 40% of students have still not found a job at all, yet alone a graduate-level position.[12]

Once you have student debt, whether or not to pay it off with savings involves comparing what you would lose to do so (something economists call the opportunity cost). Since 2012, student debt of less than £21,000 is charged interest at the level of the Retail Prices Index, which effectively just means it keeps its real value. At current rates of interest on savings, making overpayments on this could make sense (even for parents) because of the ability to drastically cut the term of the loan. However, if savings interest rates became positive (i.e. started to exceed inflation) or if superior investments are available, it would make sense to wait, invest elsewhere and ultimately use the proceeds of that investment to pay off the debt as a lump sum. Investment becomes harder to justify if there is a large student debt of over £20,000, which attracts the higher rate of RPI plus 3%. In that case, pay it off as soon as possible. Inevitably, many will not be able to, especially if they fail to reach the earnings trigger for repayment.

This is a complex area, and we can expect further tinkering with rates and debt thresholds in the years ahead. The time to think about it is at the start: take a shrewd look at your degree, where you will study, and what it will cost. Otherwise there is a chance you will end up underneath a debt cloud for much of your young adult life.

3. Home finance

Home finance is the most likely to classify as 'good debt'. While housing is nowhere near as affordable as it used to be, getting on the housing ladder usually makes sense. Those who do so tend to discover within a few years that the value of the property outgrows the mortgage debt. This creation of equity (or profit) from the purchase is one of the few pleasant financial surprises most of us can

---

12   TotalJobs website, February 2014.

rely on. Figures supplied by Nationwide going back to 1953 show an annual average increase in British property prices of 8% a year. In some areas, including London, the rise has exceeded this, while in areas which have been net losers of industry and employment, it has been much less.

Of course, these figures also conceal huge variations over time, with prices sometimes going down for four or five years at a time. But it merely emphasises that owning a house is a long-term proposition. For the purposes of multiplying your money, owning your own home is an obvious first step and getting a mortgage to fund it is clearly what we might term 'good debt'. No surprises there.

> Big house, small car – the best way to make loans pay for themselves.

Debt and inflation

Because of its dependence on land, your home is a great defence (what investors call a 'hedge') against occasional bursts of above-normal inflation, which can so damage other kinds of savings and many types of investment. Although interest rates tend to rise during inflationary times, those increased rates rarely compensate for the full effect of inflation. It is at just those times when inflation leaps that the real value of your mortgage debt will fall. If house prices rise by 10%, your salary rises by 10% and the cost of living increases by 10%, the only thing that doesn't change is the amount you owe. In real terms – that is, in your long-term ability to pay it off – the debt has diminished by 10%.[13]

You may be paying higher interest rates for a while, at least until inflation subsides, but when inflation and interest rates revert to a lower level your mortgage is still a smaller proportion of the house value than it was before, and you will get that benefit for every year

---

13 For the same reason, governments like to have a bit of inflation because it decreases the real weight of public debt. That is why government inflation targets are never zero!

of your mortgage thereafter. Inflation always helps the debtor and hurts the lender, so other things being equal more types of debt become essentially 'good' during inflationary times.

Own your home before investing

Many of those who have bought this book will already own a home and probably have a mortgage. Good – the skills required in investment are the same as those you brought to bear in buying a home. If you have not bought a home, then it is probably as well to consider doing so before embarking on investment in the markets. Although the value of the home may not always outpace your market investments (an owner-occupied home doesn't produce an income you can reinvest) the home's role as a protector against inflation is one you should cherish. Besides, you have to live somewhere, and rent will bite deeply and repeatedly into the money you hope to put away for multiplication.

Several categories of people who get housing with their jobs (some agricultural workers, caretakers, academics and medical staff) are likely to be lulled into waiting too long before getting into the property market. This is something they neglect at their peril. Very few will be able to retire in the homes that come with their jobs, and buying a house at the age of 60 or later, even if you can get a mortgage, can be a herculean undertaking. For those who can face being a landlord, buying and letting can be a useful source of income. For those who can't face it, substantial and effective saving at least equal to meeting mortgage payments would be wise. (See chapter 19 on multiplying your money with property.)

Choosing a mortgage

Just because mortgages tend to be good debts doesn't mean we should not be very careful how we choose them. Mortgages, like pensions, come in a bewildering array: variable rates, fixed rates, capped rates, discounted, flexible repayment, interest-only and so forth. Many of them tempt you to pretend to be an economist and peer into the future. What level will interest rates be at in five years' time? Will I be better off with this fixed rate than with an ordinary variable rate? If economists cannot agree on these things – and it is said that if all the economists in the world were laid end to end they would not reach a conclusion – then the ordinary consumer has little chance.

It is better perhaps to crystallise some common-sense mortgage guidelines than try to point out today's best offers, which will soon be out of date.

- Leave enough time to shop around for a mortgage: don't leave it until you have already found the home of your dreams.

- Look at the mortgage charges as well as the rates before you decide.

- Flexibility is your friend. Try to avoid products that tie you to a single provider, stop you making early capital repayments or penalise you if you want to lower them.

- In low-inflation times, pay with today's money: try to keep the loan term short, even at the cost of higher repayments.

- In high-inflation times pay with tomorrow's money: a longer repayment term is cheaper.

- Don't overreach yourself. The more you borrow as a percentage of the home cost, the higher the interest rate you will pay.

- Remortgage costs are flat rate. The larger your loan, the more sense it makes to consider a remortgage.

- Avoid exotic loans: rates tied to overseas currencies, for example, may be cheap for a while, but add an unwanted extra exchange rate variable to your finances.

- Be very sceptical of endowment-type or interest-only mortgages. If there is investment to be done, you can do it directly: it is more transparent and lower-cost, and therefore should produce higher returns.

- Always bear in mind that your lender intends to make money, however good a deal looks.

Charges are one of the biggest bugbears, and they are often larger the more unusual the type of loan you choose. Administration charges, often divided into smaller spuriously named types, can easily add up to hundreds or even thousands of pounds and not all may be disclosed when you make initial inquiries. That is particularly true when you go through comparison websites that don't have space for all the details. It is not merely the size of these fees, but the fact they are deducted from your mortgage advance before you see it. Just when you are really strapped for cash, you have to stump up the extra readies on the spot if you want the house.

If you are remortgaging, you have to account for additional overheads as if you were buying the home all over again: legal fees, valuation fees, land registry, local authority and bankruptcy searches, and the sting in the tail: the sealing fee of typically £75–100 charged by your old lender for removing their name from the deeds. Expect to pay £100 if you add or remove anyone's name from the title deed (another cost of divorce). If you fall into arrears, some banks charge you £25 for a letter telling you so, which is hardly going to make the debt easier to bear. Debt is cheaper for those who don't badly need the money, and mortgages are no exception.

For the increasing proportion of us who have irregular income, through contract work, freelance income, or casual employment, mortgages have traditionally been difficult to get, at least at anything like competitive rates. When the credit cycle is easy, it shouldn't be too hard – but when credit conditions tighten, and banks are leaned on to stop lending so freely, these are the first offers which disappear. Timing your move can be important!

The endowment debacle

Ah, another scandal. As you can see from the mortgage guidelines above, I have advised steering clear of interest-only and endowment mortgages. Fortunately, very few lenders offer them these days, because one of the few benefits of paying so much interest up front was lost when mortgage interest tax relief was abolished in 2000.

There was a time in the 1980s when 80% of new mortgages issued were endowments. The snags with them were identical to those of all with-profits products. The salesperson got almost all of the first two years' contributions, and annual management charges would eat away at subsequent investments. It would take more than seven years, on average, for the value of an endowment fund even to return the premiums paid, so appalling was the charging structure. They were inflexible in other ways, so that if you moved home and needed a bigger mortgage, you would have to get an additional policy, or a top-up repayment mortgage, all of which added to the costs and complexity. Even on those policies held to maturity, the huge weight of debt paid annually on the interest part of the loan, plus the annual charges on the investment part, would mean the lender, not the policyholder, would be the beneficiary of the compounding of investment gains.

Paying down the mortgage

Paying down any debt, even a mortgage, if you can afford it is a very effective way of multiplying your money. That is particularly true for higher-rate taxpayers, because interest is paid from taxed income. If you pay 45% tax, then a loan at 5% is actually costing you a marginal 9.1% on gross pay.

Put it another way. With a 25-year £125,000 mortgage at 5%, paying off a tenth of it right at the start will save you four and a half years on the term, and £26,400 in interest. (See Figure 7.2.)

Before you plan a capital repayment you should certainly check your mortgage conditions. Watch out for redemption penalties and the minimum lump sums acceptable. Also check to see when your lender calculates the sum owing. Some do this only once a year, so if you paid in your lump sum a couple of days after that, you would waste a year's interest. Whatever you decide to do, tell your mortgage provider what you are planning, and make doubly sure they know that the sum is intended as a capital repayment not an advance on interest owed (why anyone would make an advance payment on interest I do not know). Obviously, if you are on a low fixed-rate mortgage, it would make sense to hold your lump-sum repayment until the loan reverts to a market rate.

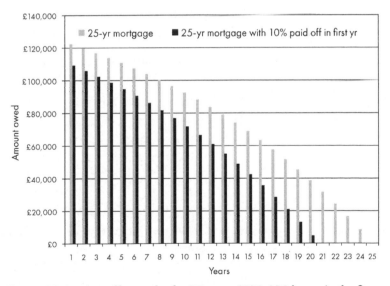

Figure 7.2. Paying off a tenth of a 25-year £125,000 home in the first year

The total cost drops by the area between the two curves, a tremendous return if you can manage it.

Credit, debit and charge cards

Where would we be without credit, debt and charge cards? Of the three, credit cards offer the greatest benefits but the greatest drawbacks because of the invitation to run up debt. (Charge cards, such as American Express, have to be paid off in full each month, while debit cards only work when you have money in the bank account they link to.)

The key point to remember with credit cards is that being unable to repay in full is going to cost you dear. The interest rates are high and mercilessly applied. If you don't pay off every penny you will generally be charged interest on the *whole* bill, not just the part you didn't pay. You also pay interest on items that fall in the new billing period up to the next statement date. On top of this you could incur a hefty charge, typically £15–20, if you didn't make the stated minimum payment, which is usually 5% of the bill. If you are in danger of getting into debt, an arranged loan or overdraft with your bank to pay the card off will usually work out much cheaper.

If you do get hit with charges, try complaining. Like banks, credit card companies want to keep your custom, particularly if you have been with them for a while. If you normally pay off your entire balance, but just missed this once, most card companies are usually willing to refund the interest and charges. The same is true of annual fees. At the time of writing, most card companies refund them for those who spend a certain amount on the card.

Don't forget to check through those free services that come with some credit cards: purchase protection insurance, dispute resolution and frequent flier points, for example.

Conclusion

- Tackle debt early, never let it build unchecked.

- Loan rates matter.

- Choose good debt over bad: big house, small car!

- Invest in the right kind of education.

- High inflation is kind to the borrower.

- Low inflation is kind to the lender.

- Shop around, check the small print.

- Build in flexibility.

- Own the home you live in.

- Don't get stung by credit cards.

Once we have clear ideas of where we can save money and have got a grasp of our debts, the savings should come trickling in. Next we need to organise our savings into two types: money we will put away to start multiplying and money that is a cushion for unexpected events. The best way to start organising on those lines is tackled in the next chapter.

CHAPTER 8.
Organising Your Savings

Introduction

THE GLOBAL FINANCIAL CRISIS OF 2007–8 WAS A MORTAL SHOCK to those of us who had grown up with the idea that banks never fail. We will never see them, or indeed other financial institutions, the same way again. This has profound implications for the risks of investment, as we will see in chapter 9, but also for savings. The vision of thousands of people queuing to remove their savings from Northern Rock made us realise that without state guarantees, even our savings could be lost.

Yet the instinct to save is undiminished, even if the resources to do it are. In some ways we are better off now because we now realise the risks that were actually always there. In the US, where small banks fail quite frequently, consumers are more used to the idea. In Britain, Northern Rock was the first bank to fail since 1866. This chapter will help you organise your surplus cash into the places where it meets your needs best.

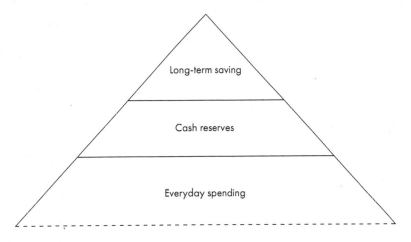

Figure 8.1: The money pyramid

The largest amount of your disposable income is going to be eaten up by the costs of daily living. The next slice needs to be available quickly in case of unexpected events or an emergency, and what is left can be invested long term at the best returns you can manage.

Organising your savings

This chapter is concerned with the middle slice of the pyramid in the diagram above. The size of cash reserves you should look to build depends on personal circumstances. Ironically, the better off you are the less you will need. Those who are well-paid often have access to low-cost loans through either an arranged overdraft or a company loan through an employer, and may have an array of almost liquid investments which can be sold at short notice. The better off are also better able to repay any short-term debt they need to incur.

Those who have low or unreliable incomes and big fixed outgoings do not have these advantages, and need fairly cast-iron provisions for the unexpected. Failure to make them, and lack of access to cheap forms of finance, are some of the main reasons that many less well-off people find themselves dragged into debt by circumstances.

Whatever amount you do set aside as cash reserves should gradually diminish as a proportion of your savings: first, because your investments are growing, and secondly because increasing assets will open up other avenues of finance.

Liquidity

Liquidity is an important idea. It means how quickly a particular asset can be turned into cash when you need it. Liquidity and rate of return pull in opposite directions, so the most liquid assets like cash or current accounts tend to earn you much less than your home, pension or a selection of stocks and shares. However, it is worth noting that some items – like a flexible mortgage, which allows you to underpay (or overpay) and switch the cash to other uses, and some pensions, like the stakeholder, add to your liquidity because you can stop contributing without penalty. Obviously, both have their costs and limitations, but may well be preferable to selling shares or investment funds in some market conditions.

Lack of liquidity can really cost us dear. In the 1970s and 80s, millions of people who committed to long-term with-profits insurance policies intended to run for 20 or 25 years cashed them in or stopped contributing within the first five years. Usually the reason was to raise cash quickly, but in most cases the bulk of contributions was lost, together with all gains, past, present and future. Selling a long-term investment before it has a chance to grow is as wasteful as using a Rembrandt to plug a leaking roof. A little cash put by for emergency roof repairs and similar needs can give us greater confidence that long-term investments can be left alone to do their job (see Figure 8.1).

Thinking the unthinkable

Needing a large amount of money unexpectedly and immediately is fairly rare. Some of the biggest financial outlays, such as school fees or residential care for an elderly relative, can often be planned for some time ahead, and indeed can be one of the reasons we are planning to multiply our money in the first place. Some events, such as serious road accidents or having to give up work to care for a disabled child, are emotional disasters first and financial second. Although they can overwhelm the finances of even the well-off, they are relatively rare. Divorce, too, is an emotional and financial disaster, and far from rare, as we saw in chapter 6. There may be mortgage protection policies for disability or job loss, but there is nothing to offset the wrench of a marital split. Clearly, investing time and effort in a marriage can pay tremendous returns both emotionally and financially.

Bank and savings accounts

Once you have decided how big your reserves need to be, you need to decide where to put them. The banking scene has become a lot more confusing in recent years, with internet-based competitors that arrived amid great razzmatazz and then generally sank into the background without fulfilling their potential. Most internet-based accounts now are being operated by jazzy new subsidiaries of traditional high-street banks. As customers, it is more important than ever to keep an eye on our banks, because keener competition is manifest in faster changes in products and sometimes worse terms or rates for the services we use. If it isn't cash-machine charges it will be charges for using the branch cashiers, or it might be poorer rates on deposits. And you never want to have more than £85,000 (or £170,000 for joint accounts) in any one bank or with any single firm, because that is the limit guaranteed under the Financial Services Compensation Scheme.

A few guidelines can easily be distilled:

- Think 'convenience' for banking and 'interest' for savings.

- Pay more attention to charges than to interest rates on a current account.

- Don't let excessive amounts sit earning low interest: park your savings in high-interest accounts.

- Don't tie your savings up for years in fixed-interest products: they are usually publicised most at the bottom of the interest-rate cycle.

- Monitor the terms and conditions of existing accounts frequently: they often change, and rarely for the better.

- Don't take dubious charges lying down. Contest them.

Banking in Britain, even after the financial crisis, is an extremely profitable business. High charges, low interest rates on many accounts, changes in conditions without adequate notice, all combine to make banks a lot of money. But the biggest boost to profits is customer inertia. Apparently, we Britons are more likely to change our spouses than our bankers. We grumble and we moan, but all too few of us do anything about it.

In fact, it really isn't hard to change your bank account any more, and you should at least threaten to do it from time to time, just to keep your bank on its toes. There is an industry code of practice now which means that standing orders and direct debits can be quickly transferred from the old bank to the new, together with the money.

If you have been wrongly charged, don't take it lying down. Phone the bank call centre and make a fuss. Threaten to leave. Nine times out of ten you will get your money back, even if the charge turns out to be legitimate ("Just this once, because you are a long-standing customer," is what they often say).

Banks often use a business model that divides customers into those who are cost and interest-rate sensitive and those who are not. When a new savings account is launched, let us call it ABC GoldOne, it will be heavily publicised for all its bonus interest rates, low charges and so forth, and garner thousands of new customers. For six months or so the bank keeps these rates in place, but then gradually eases back the savings rates, slips in new charges and generally makes that account far less competitive than it used to be. At the same time it will launch another new account, ABC PlatinumOne, with rates as good as GoldOne's used to be.

The rate-sensitive customers, those that tutted their way through the changing small print of GoldOne, and were on the point of leaving ABC bank altogether, then switch to PlatinumOne, while those who don't read the new terms and conditions are blithely thinking they are still getting a good deal. Those who are reluctant to switch are the real goldmine of banking, and bankers love them with all their hearts.[14]

As far as a current account is concerned, your average balance should be only enough to accommodate the bills that flow out of it from the pay that comes in. Excess money should be moved regularly to where it makes a better rate. Some banks now have a tool called a sweep, which allows you to automatically sweep into a savings account any excess in your current account above a certain sum.

Certainly, you shouldn't have enough money in a current account to care whether it offers 0.1% or 1% a year, so long as it offers you the convenience you need without charges for cash machines or other services. If your net pay of, say, £1,500 a month goes into your current account and you have none left at the end of the average month, your average balance may be around £750. Over a year, your

---

14   Incidentally, this business model can also crop up anywhere where product offerings are complex or bundled in different ways. Insurance renewals are a classic case. Just this week while writing this book I saved £100 with a single phone call by challenging my home insurance renewal premium.

1% on that is barely going to buy you a takeaway curry for one. But just one month's unauthorised overdraft fee can be £20–£30.

Some banks offer combined accounts, with reasonable savings rates and fairly good banking services. They are worth looking into for those whose savings are likely to be less than a couple of thousand pounds, but those with more savings can usually do better.

National Savings

National Savings exists as a mechanism for the government to tap the savings of its citizens. As long as you keep that in mind, you won't be surprised that the attractiveness of these savings products is so variable.

Normally, during those times that the government is running a big deficit and desperately needs your hard-earned cash to help fund the gap between public spending and what it gets in taxes, it will pay quite handsomely to borrow your money. The previous edition of this book covered NS&I offers in some detail. But right now, there is only one product that is very attractive: one and three-year pensioner bonds, only for the over-65s, but offering interest rates respectively of 2.8 and 4%, well above most competing products. Younger readers should also keep an eye out for new products. NS&I has in the past been quite innovative, and may be so in the future.

Conclusion

We need conventional savings accounts for our short-term cash reserves. Naturally, look for the highest interest available combined with quick access. Those accounts that offer telephone or internet transfers and bill payment mechanisms are often the most convenient, allowing us to keep the money earning interest until the last minute. The Saturday edition of the *Financial Times* has a section called databank, which shows the latest best rates, as do some of the other broadsheets.

Here is a quick summary:

- Use the money pyramid to separate your cash into three.

- Keep everyday cash in a convenient low-charge bank account for day-to-day spending.

- Cash reserves should earn high interest with immediate access.

- Put the rest to work for the long term.

- Watch for changing conditions on your bank and savings accounts.

For the savings which we are prepared to commit for the long term, we have loftier ambitions. You may recall from chapter 2 that the UK stock market has averaged an annual 5.1% real return since 1899, roughly 7–8% before inflation. We are aiming at least to match that. The next chapter will start to show you how.

CHAPTER 9.
Taking on the Markets

Introduction

S O FAR WE HAVE STAYED IN THE FINANCIAL MAINSTREAM. BANK
accounts, mortgages, consumer debt, even pensions, are
things we all have to deal with at some stage in life. But now
we are ready to move up a gear and look into new and forbidding
territory: welcome to the stock market, where the money is really
made.

However, before we step in we need to dispel a few myths:

- ordinary people should stay out of stock markets

- beginners don't have any financial skills

- all the money is made by experts

- shares are risky

- shares won't perform so well in the future as in the past

- my money is safer in the bank.

We're already in!

Some of these can be easily dealt with. Almost all of us already have a stake in the stock market. If we have an occupational pension, an endowment mortgage, or a with-profits life-insurance policy, we are already investing indirectly in many hundreds if not thousands of shares and gilt-edged stocks. As for not having financial skills, how can that be said of anyone who owns their own home? The stress and complexities of buying a house make investing in shares a doddle.

Experts do make money, yes, but those running big investment funds face problems that you and I do not when trying to turn good judgement into good returns. In fact, if you ask investment experts to look after your money the chances are that after charges they will make less than if you did it yourself.

As for shares being risky, that depends on how you approach them. History shows that a broad portfolio of shares, held for the long term, will outperform all other investments. There will be years in which the market as a whole falls by 5% or 10%, but there will also be years in which they rise by 15% or 20% (and history shows these rising years are more common). In the long term, money is certainly not safer in a bank.

> The average person, appropriately prepared and reasonably cautious, can make money in the stock market.

That isn't to say we should all immediately rush out and buy individual shares. Many people, particularly those with no interest in how marketplaces operate, or no spare time, will simply opt for fund investments. (If you know already that this is what you want to do, chapter 11 shows you how to get the best value for money.) Nevertheless, it is important to know how the average person, appropriately prepared and reasonably cautious, can make money in the stock market. Of course, the fund management industry wants you to believe otherwise, just as painters and decorators want to discourage you from putting up your own wallpaper, just as plumbers have horror stories about people who plumbed in their own washing machine, just as builders shake their heads and tut when they hear you put a room in the loft single-handedly.

Yes, we can make mistakes, but so can the experts. The difference is that for us, our own financial well-being is priority number one, two and three. Commission never gets a look in. When we run our own investments, losses and inefficiencies come to light quickly. We can rethink our strategies. Yet the professional who had his commission up front often has no incentive to draw your attention to investment mistakes, and they can lie undiscovered for years or even decades.

Look at the scandals of the past 20 years: Equitable Life, personal pensions mis-selling, home income mis-selling, endowment mis-selling, the global financial crisis, and plain old everyday overcharging. There are just as many crooks and bodgers in financial services as there are in the building industry. Just because they wear suits, don't mean they ain't cowboys.

What is so peculiar about investment is the way it is wrapped up in a kind of mythology and a deliberately obscure language. It isn't like a set of kitchen cupboards that we notice a builder fitted upside down, or the copper pipes we spot behind the shower when the plumber billed us for chrome. We don't hesitate to check up on these, often matters of a few tenners here and there. Yet when it comes to a with-profits fund which is worth no more now than seven years ago, we often hold fire, even though the amount of money lost can be equivalent to having a wallet stolen every Friday night for a year. The truth is that many of us feel nervous about querying a life-insurance company or a bank because we are out of our depth, as if we are interrogating a priest over the nature of divinity.

There is a great deal of expertise in the investment industry, but for too long its priorities have not coincided with those of customers.

Now, with the broadening array and falling cost of tracker funds, exchange-traded funds and self-invested personal pensions, there is a real chance for the public to get value for money. What we have to do is make sure we are actively looking for it.

Discovering your investment skills

Becoming your own financial expert may sound daunting, but it shouldn't. Anyone who has ever bought a home has already demonstrated all the skills required, and in a far more stressful and demanding environment. There is nothing about investing in the stock markets that comes anywhere near the sheer agony of dealing with a housing chain, sniffy solicitors and evasive estate agents. Look at all the things involved in being a first time buyer:

- comparing the cost of buying with renting

- deciding on an area, not only as a place to live but also whether it is on its way up or down

- timing your purchase to take account of the state of the housing market

- working out how big a mortgage you can afford

- deciding between a fixed and variable interest rate

- finding the right home in your chosen area

- haggling over the price and assessing how keenly others want it

- dealing with expensive legal and property professionals

- making sure the seller really owns the property, has not got a secret second mortgage, and that it won't fall down

- once finally moved in, subsisting for the first six months on baked beans and wondering if you will ever be able to afford carpets or furniture.

Let's face it, if this were a share purchase it would be the trickiest transaction going. Every ordinary share in BP or GlaxoSmithKline is exactly the same as every other one, but every home is different. Even when homes are similar, location has a huge impact on value. There is no annual report or investor material to make sure you know what you are getting until you order a surveyor's report and solicitor's questions. The dividend for owning a home is the value of living in the place, but just like a share, you are really hoping for substantial capital gains too. Transaction charges on buying a home probably amount to 4–5% of its value, compared with 1–1.5% with shares.

Finally, if you get a mortgage you have blithely agreed to borrow anything up to 90% of the value of an asset that can easily fluctuate in value by more than 10% in a year. The equivalent position in share trading is spread betting, rightly labelled as high-risk.

The curse of the short-term view

The reason that a house purchase seems so safe, despite all the overheads, the debt burden and the stress involved, while share markets are seen as risky, is purely one of perspective. People often live in their homes for many years, unaware of whether they are worth more or less than they paid for them. However, the perspective on shares and other investments, fanned by the press, always seems to be less than a year and everyone pays an inordinate amount of attention to the price, sometimes on a daily basis.

We will look at this in greater detail later on, but suffice it to say, if you enter the share market with the same long-term time frame as when you buy a house, and spread your investments prudently, you can afford to be just as sanguine about short-term price movements.

Investments to suit your needs

Before you begin investing you need to decide what you want your investments to do for you. Would you prefer to settle for a low but steady rate of growth, without much volatility, or are you looking for strong growth, even if that comes with a big-dipper kind of ride? How do you feel about risk? Are you looking to take a regular income from your investments, or are you happy to see all the returns ploughed back in for future growth? If you want to multiply your money, you will recall from chapter 1 that investing for long-term capital growth with all dividends and income reinvested is the best way to achieve it. But even if you have a shorter-term view, or need to tap your investments for cash to live on, there is still something to be said for capital growth. Let's look at the issues involved, starting with risk.

Weighing up risk

Nothing in life is without risk, but assessing and comparing risk levels is something we are often not too good at. Many years ago, I overheard two middle-aged women tutting over something. As I listened more closely one inhaled deeply from her cigarette, snorted out a plume of thick blue smoke and said hoarsely to the other: "You know, I'm not sure I can risk eating beef again with all this BSE about."

Familiar risks, whether it be smoking-related diseases or road accidents, seem less unsettling to us than unfamiliar risks like BSE, even when those unfamiliar risks are only one ten-thousandth as likely to happen. When most people talk about risk they just mean the chance and the extent of the bad things happening. In investing, I will define risk as a departure from expected returns upwards or downwards. In investing, the big rewards and the big disappointments are always two sides of the same coin. You can't hide your savings from the downside of share investments without losing the upside. Never believe anyone who tells you there is a quick, low-risk route to becoming wealthy. It doesn't exist. There is a long and steady one, however, which is what this book is all about.

The small print at the bottom of every investment fund advertisement rightly warns you "The value of shares can go down as well as up." But stitched on the underside of every mattress should be a warning too: "Money put here can *only* go down in value." The same, after the effects of inflation, is true of bank current accounts. What I'm getting at is that the biggest risk is incurred by *not* being in the market. Nothing matches shares for return in the long term, as we saw in chapter 2.

So is the stock market a risky place to put your money in any other way? Well, yes and no. If you buy shares in one single company, there is some chance that the company will go bankrupt, the ultimate bad event which could leave your investment worth nothing at all. It is worth remembering that there is never any guarantee, however much investment homework you do, that a company cannot go bankrupt. Barings, one of the most conservatively run and famous names in British banking, which had weathered world wars, coups, and every kind of market crash in its 200-year history, was destroyed in 1995 by the actions of one single, panicking trader, playing ever larger double-or-quits market bets.

The same is true of big profit drops. The highly paid investment analysts who eat and breathe the companies they follow are often as surprised as everyone else by these shocks.

But the risks work in the other direction too. Not too many people in 1982 would have bet that a small company run by a college dropout with a bad haircut would in less than 20 years end up with its products on almost every desk in every home and office in the developed world. Bill Gates made it and literally thousands of other businessmen didn't. This is the other side of the risk coin. Share prices are effectively a barometer of investment feeling about a company, drawing a wavy middle line between those two possibilities of triumph and disaster. (For more about risk, and the many ways investors can minimise it, see chapter 12.)

Risk, time and perspective

The final cushion against risk is quite simply time. Suppose a share goes up 10% a year on average, but in half of those years it goes down by 5% and in the other half goes up by 15%. There is a greater risk of that share being a disappointing investment if your investment horizon is a year than if it is ten years. If you look at a long-term share price chart of the FTSE 100, it looks like shares have just oscillated since 1999, but that chart ignores the reinvested dividends, which are the most important part of share returns. The real post-inflation return over that period is about 4.5% a year, which beats most things for which we have data.

Concentrating risk

So far we have dealt with the ways of fighting risk by spreading it, offsetting it and taking the long view. There is another view, exactly the opposite: to home in specifically on areas you know well, hoping that your unsurpassed knowledge will allow you to spot the big opportunities and step aside before trouble arrives.

Professional investment traders often do very well with their own personal bets in such volatile areas as futures, traded options, spread betting, and contracts for differences (these are defined in the glossary). But even they can get caught out by aligning their living with their investments. It is worth expanding a little on these kinds of risk.

A professional market analyst may very well be able to spot good individual investments in such volatile markets as Russia, Indonesia and so forth; indeed, the temptations to make personal trades for those who recommend such deals for a living must be almost irresistible. The profits can be superb for a while, tempting the investment of ever-larger sums, but when the investment tide turns it can do so very sharply. Not only might our professional lose his job because no one wants to buy emerging markets stocks, but his savings (invested in those stocks) may have halved in value too.

These kinds of twinned risks are also run by those families which have gone into business together, and individuals whose wealth is tied up in stock options with their employer. Think of the unfortunate Northern Rock employees who in 2007 had pensions, shares, car loans and cut-price mortgages with their employer. When the bank was rescued, many lost their jobs, savings and perks they had come to rely on, all in one go.

Income or capital growth?

The conventional wisdom for many years has been that you should try to increase the value of your capital until you retire, and then switch to investments which pay a good income but do not increase much in value. In a sense what you will have manufactured is an annuity, and because the average person is living so much longer these days (as shown in chapter 3), it will have the same disadvantages.

In fact, investors should probably delay a switch to income until many years after retirement because in the medium term, a good capital-growth fund or portfolio may produce more income than an income-based portfolio, just as a fast-growing company with a low but increasing dividend may produce more income than a static company with a large but static dividend.

In Figure 9.1, assume each share cost £1 in the first year. The slow firm pays 6p, a 6% yield on your £1 invested, and the dividend rises by 5% a year. The fast-growing company only pays 2p a year, a 2% yield, but the dividend rises at 30% a year, in line with the shares. By year six, the utility's dividend is matched by the growth share, then soon much-surpassed. And then you consider the capital value of the investment! By year ten the growth share is worth £5.16 and the utility £1.20.

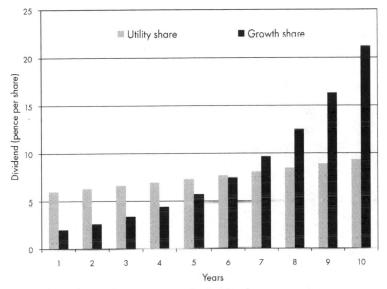

Figure 9.1. Big dividends vs growth dividends

A comparison of dividends: take two shares, each costing 100p. One is a utility paying a 6p dividend, a 6% yield, and the other a growing company which pays 2p, a 2% yield. However, while the utility dividend is raised 5% a year, the growth dividend is increased 30%. After ten years the growth investor has received 85p in total income, almost 10p more than the utility investor.

For those who need income from their investments within a very few years, chapter 21 on bonds is a good place to start. As long as your investments are performing well, you can always turn some of that increase in capital growth into income by selling so long as you don't mind it being a little irregular. The convenience of an ISA, for example, is that you can withdraw funds whenever you wish, free of tax. Naturally, by raiding your investment, you are breaking one of the three basic rules which help you multiply your money, so the bigger the bites you take from it the less well it will grow in the future.

Conclusion

- Don't underestimate your own skills.

- Investing is easier than buying a home.

- You really can beat the professionals.

- Cutting out the middleman will save you money too.

- Investment risk and investment return go hand in hand.

- The biggest risk is staying out of the markets.

- Time is the great antidote to market fluctuations.

- Don't switch to income-based investment too early.

CHAPTER 10.

The Simple Way to Multiply Your Money

Introduction

THIS REALLY COULD BE THE SHORTEST CHAPTER IN THE BOOK. IT is for those who are happy to ditch all of the time and effort of getting to know individual shares, of monitoring them, and of sharing their joys and sorrows. Instead, we are going the collective funds route, to see which are good and which are bad, and whether the services of an investment professional are worth having. What we are looking for is a return which – if not quite as good as the best that individual share picking has to offer – will still be decent, close to the 5.1% overall real return that the market has made historically, and low-maintenance in terms of time and charges.

The solution is as follows:

- find two or three broad market trackers which charge 0.25% a year or less

- make sure there are no initial charges

- spread them between an ISA and a SIPP

- pile in money on a regular monthly basis

- reinvest the dividends

- watch the money multiply.

The rest of the chapter is about explaining this conclusion. By the end of it you will know what a fund is, the difference between passive and active investment, how a unit trust differs from an investment trust, and why it is that highly paid fund managers cannot beat the market averages.

What are investment funds?

There are a thousand and one types of funds which will make the investment decision on your behalf, although choosing among them is at least as difficult as choosing shares. Essentially, they all pool the money of thousands of investors, giving the benefits of participation in a broad spectrum of hundreds of shares or other assets which it would be uneconomic for an individual investor to own.

There are three main types of fund. First, there are passive funds. These own a representative sample of the shares included in an index, such as the FTSE 100 or FTSE All-Share, and do no more than aim to mimic, or track, its performance. So, if the FTSE 100 increases by 8.6% in a year, you can be certain that a FTSE 100 tracker fund, before charges, will be pretty close to that figure.

The second type are active funds, which use professional money managers actively to pick and choose a collection of shares on a certain theme, whether it be UK growth or Far Eastern recovery, or South American telecommunications. Active funds aim to do better than the market as a whole, although on average they do not succeed.

Finally, there are exchange-traded funds (ETFs), which are like passive funds, but constructed as single shares which can be bought or sold on stock markets. These are highly liquid funds which allow individuals to cost-effectively access areas like emerging markets and commodities.

Why you can beat the professionals

All of the active funds literature will show you graphs and tables of how well they have done over the last one, five and ten years. In the small print, somewhere, will be the soubriquet: "Past performance is not necessarily a guide to future performance." This is true except for one word: "necessarily". In fact, over the long term both outperforming and underperforming funds tend to revert to the average of all funds. This led to an amusing series of articles in US financial newspaper the *Wall Street Journal*, in which the stock picks of a monkey (actually I think it was really a journalist, but having been one for more than a decade I can understand how the two were confused) throwing darts at a list of shares attached to a dartboard frequently outperformed professional money managers who earned millions of dollars a year.

Why is it, then, that investment professionals, spending all day looking at their Bloomberg screens, spending long lunchtimes tucking into lobster thermidor with the directors of Fat Bank Plc, and their evenings poring over annual reports, cannot beat the market averages? The answer is a mathematical truth as well as a common-sense one. *The average fund manager must in the long term return an average performance, because that is what averages measure.*

The average fund manager could only perform better than the average investor if there were a category of investor, perhaps the small private shareholder, who was constantly getting saddled with worse-than-average performance. In fact, the shareholdings of investment institutions – the pension funds, insurance companies, investment banks, unit trusts and investment trusts – make up an overwhelming proportion of the total value of the market, so for them to do even slightly better than the average, private investors would have to do *much* worse. Yet there is no evidence that is the case.

So why are investment professionals paid such vast salaries and year-end bonuses if they are unable to do any better choosing which shares to buy or sell than you or I could by throwing darts at the share tables of the *Financial Times*? Good question: all we can do is make sure it isn't our money.

The inbuilt inefficiencies of the professionals

Let's be sympathetic here. Fund managers have to cope with a whole raft of problems that don't affect small investors. To begin with, there are the problems of success. The better a fund performs, the more investors pile in, and the more money under management it gets. That may bring some managerial economies, just like a half-million-tonne supertanker run with the same number of crew as a hundred-thousand-tonne tanker, but like the supertanker changes in direction take longer and produce some big waves. Big funds need millions of shares in each of their investments to be economic, and getting hold of them is likely to push up the price. Similarly, getting out of a badly performing stock is pretty easy if you only own a hundred shares, but if it is ten million you will find yourself selling into a falling market. Why does this happen? Quite simply because the amount you are selling will have soaked up all the available buyers at the current price, and the price will need to drop somewhat for you to entice in other buyers.

Professional traders always try to sniff out what funds are buying or selling, just as hyenas will track a pride of lions in search of a free meal at the end. This is a pain for the fund manager because other buyers piling in push up the price, just as it is a pain for the lions, who might end up having to share their kill. Fund managers go to great lengths to disguise what they are trading, often spreading their biggest deals between a number of brokers to avoid letting other market participants know what they are buying or selling, and waiting for the maximum time before disclosing their shareholdings to the regulatory authorities.

There are some other dynamics that hinder fund managers too, and explain a lot about the variability of returns. One is that specialist funds, such as those investing in biotechnology or high-technology start-ups, often find it hard to attract substantial numbers of investors until their target market is already fashionable. That means that by the time the average investor gets to hear about the fund, the track record looks excellent, but those first, and often best, years of growth will be behind it. The initial biotechnology entrepreneurs will have sold stakes to the venture capitalists, who will have made a tidy sum and sold to the specialist funds, and then the wider public arrives just as the whole sector is really expensive and ripe for a fall.

Then there are the problems of failure. A fund that is performing very badly will tend to suffer a cash outflow as investors cut their losses. If it is a unit trust, investors sell back their units to the fund, and the fund must come up with the cash. This can be very awkward, and involve selling investments at a loss when the fund manager is convinced they could come good in the long term. At the very least it leaves the fund stuck with yesterday's poorly performing stocks and shares, and with insufficient cash to search out new bargains. So managers of active funds have a hard time of it to turn whatever stock-picking and market experience they have into an enduring market-beating performance. Yet the average charges for an active fund are 4-5% of an initial investment (i.e. £400–500 on £10,000 invested) and an annual fee of 1 or 2% on the value of the fund, i.e. £100–200 at the end of the first year, and if the fund rose 10% then £110–220 at the end of the second.

In the era of fund supermarkets, not too many people have to pay the initial charge, but some still do. And the follow on costs alone are enough to eat up a quarter of all your contributions over 25 years. This is an extremely high price to pay for average performance, and makes a huge difference to long-term returns (see Figure 10.1). Some of the handicaps are self-inflicted. Many of these so-called active funds are 'closet trackers' with rules enforcing an almost market weighting of any stock, whatever the fund manager's opinion of it. It seems fund companies are so scared of underperforming the market that they remove any hope of seriously outperforming. From the investor's point of view, it is pretty unimpressive to pay so much and still not be able to weed out the obvious underperforming sectors.

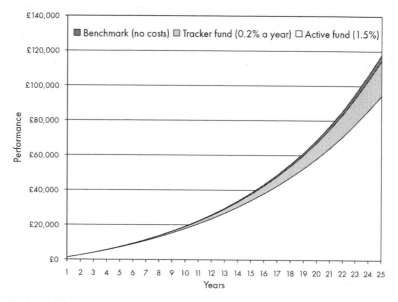

Figure 10.1. Why 1.5% is a very large number

Comparison of the performance over 25 years of two funds returning 10% a year from £100 per month contributions. The highest line shows the benchmark performance with no costs. The second line shows the performance of a tracker fund charging 0.2% a year, and the lowest shows that of an active fund with a 1.5% charge. The active fund charges swallow up £23,700 – equal to more than three quarters of total contributions.

This section may be summarised as follows:

- The average managed fund will by definition perform averagely, as measured by market indices.

- Individual outperformance and underperformance are temporary; funds in the long term tend to revert to the average.

- Past performance will not help an investor to pick an outperforming fund.

- From an investor's perspective, investment in a managed fund underperforms the market average in the long term by the amount of its fees.

- Fund managers' knowledge and skills are offset by the size inefficiencies inherent to institutional investing.

Passive funds: getting average returns cheaply

So, if it is difficult to avoid getting average returns, perhaps we should just try to get them as cheaply as possible. Trackers have no grander aim than to produce average returns, but because they do not need an investment research staff and require only minimal management they tend to be quite cheap. Many UK-based trackers currently charge no initial fee, and less than 1% and sometimes as little as 0.1% of the value of the fund each year.

A fund tracking the FTSE 100 would use a computer to buy shares in the top 100 UK companies in the same proportion as they appear in the index. When the index is revised, the tracker sells the shares that are no longer included and buys the new entrants.

If you are new to investing, and reluctant to research and buy individual shares yourself, a low-cost FTSE 100 or FTSE All-Share tracker fund is a good place to start. It is easy to understand and cheap to run, and can safely be forgotten about from one month end to the next, knowing that it will produce market average returns of 7–8% nominal, enough to double your money every ten years. Tracker funds can be used as the investment engine inside most personal pensions and ISAs, as well as on their own. Most tracker funds are constructed as a type of unit trust, so let us take a closer look at them.

Unit trusts and OEICs

Unit trusts are what are known as open-ended investment vehicles. That means they can expand to accept all the money that is subscribed to them by issuing new units and making fresh investments. By contrast a closed fund, like an investment trust, only has a certain number of shares, and you can only buy from someone who is selling. If you subscribe to a unit trust, your money is pooled with contributions from others and used to buy investments. Instead of share certificates, you have a statement of the number of units you own and the price of those units. You multiply one by the other to get the value of your investments (if the statement has not already done that). You can find out what your units are worth at any time online or in the managed funds sections of broadsheet newspapers.

Open-ended investment companies (OEICs) are simply unit trusts structured as companies, allowing them to sell their services across Europe. The only difference an investor will notice is that there is no bid–offer spread on the sale and purchase of units, and an initial charge is levied instead.

Investment trusts

Investment trusts are companies that buy stakes in other companies, and their shares are quoted on the London Stock Exchange. There are a few hundred of them and they have come back into favour recently because of their flexibility. Most of them are actively managed, and have a particular geographic or market sector focus.

The major difference between investment trusts and unit trusts is that investment trusts can borrow money. They can do so either by issuing various classes of stock (either debentures or zero dividend preference shares) or through bank loans. This means investment trusts have the opportunity to buy shares on margin (i.e. part funded by borrowing), just as a mortgage means we can buy a £300,000 home for a £30,000 deposit. When prices are rising, this allows them to get better returns, but when shares go in the opposite direction it will magnify any losses.

Another major difference compared with unit trusts is that the share price of investment trusts is not a precise valuation of all the underlying assets minus any debts (known as net asset value). The share price, just as in any quoted company, fluctuates. In the case of an investment trust it reflects not only the supply and demand for the shares, but also market perceptions of the management and its chosen investment field. Most investment trusts trade at a discount to their net asset value, a situation which has persisted for some years. The important conclusion to draw is not that you are getting a bargain by buying at less than net asset value, but what the underlying trend in overall net asset value is.

Obviously a fund that grows its assets rapidly will see an increase in its share price, even if a discount to net asset value persists. The only time when a discount would be important is if a trust is taken over by another company or fund, when holders are likely to be offered much closer to the true value of the assets.

ISAs

ISAs or individual savings accounts were introduced in 1999, and followed on from a similar scheme called the personal equity plan (PEP). The idea is to encourage individual share ownership by giving a yearly allowance that can be protected against capital gains tax and any additional tax on dividend income (share dividends are paid net of a 10% tax, though most bonds are paid gross). There was also a separate class of cash ISA, for savers. In the 2014 Budget, these were combined into a new ISA (NISA), so that you can put £15,000 a year (2014/15) into either stocks and shares or cash, fully protected from tax. This is a big boost for savers, who could previously only put in £5,760. There are also plans to launch a peer-to-peer lending ISA in a couple of years (see chapter 12 for more about P2P).

The cheapest way to buy an active fund

Most people who make a fund investment use an ISA or a SIPP as a tax-wrapper. The easiest way to compare funds is at an online funds supermarket, many of which will offer no-load funds (those without an initial charge). They may also be the cheapest place to go, so long as you don't need advice – and you won't get impartial advice from the financial advisor at a fund manager anyway. Most will rebate the entire upfront sales commission, as do most online stockbrokers. Do check the other costs.

Exchange-traded funds

Exchange-traded funds (ETFs) are the johnny-come-lately of the investment scene, but have soared in popularity in the last decade. They are now worth $450 billion worldwide. ETFs allow individuals to buy and sell whole baskets of securities as a single share, with very low fees. Unlike most funds, you can buy as few or as many as you want, and fees can be as low as 0.07%. Like investment trusts, ETFs weren't recommended by most advisors until recently, because they don't pay commission. This commission-led approach was outlawed a couple of years ago, and both ETFs and investment trusts have benefitted.

However, one particular issue with ETFs, more than with other funds, is that of counter-party risk. Some ETFs don't have a physical holding of the investment they are offering, but have taken derivative contracts to offer an exposure to it. Ever since the collapse of Lehman Brothers in 2008, investors have worried that such derivative contracts which are an intrinsic part of some funds such as guaranteed equity bonds and some ETFs, can be nullified if the counterparty taking the risk goes into default. Moreover, many ETFs are traded 'off exchange' between major fund groups dealing directly or via a specialist broker. This doesn't help the transparency of the sector. Nonetheless, ETFs are a useful addition to the low-cost toolset of the passive investor.

Conclusion

If you want a quiet life, are not particularly interested in investment, yet still want to multiply your money for the long term, subscribing to a collection of low-cost trackers or perhaps some carefully selected ETFs in an ISA or SIPP is the simplest and most effective form of investment.

- Low charges mean almost all of the market's rise finds its way into your pocket.

- A collective fund means you never have to think about the ups and downs of an individual company.

- Leaving your investments for a minimum of a decade means the market's inevitable boom and bust cycles will not trouble you.

CHAPTER 11.

How to Buy Shares

Introduction

ONCE YOU HAVE DECIDED TO BUY SHARES IN INDIVIDUAL companies you need to know a little of the mechanics of how to do it and where to get the information on which to base your decisions. Start gradually, follow a few shares to begin with and you will soon be ready to make your first trade.

This chapter shows you how to:

- have fun setting up a portfolio with imaginary money

- understand the financial pages

- find the reasons why share prices move

- choose a stockbroker

- trade with confidence

- research companies

- interpret basic financial data

- build a share portfolio which spreads risk.

First steps

If you are new to investing in shares, the easiest way to get to know the ropes is to spend a few months with an imaginary portfolio. It is obviously far better to make any early mistakes with pretend money!

Award yourself a portfolio of £100,000 and divide it among ten shares that you like the look of. The simplest way is to set an online watchlist or portfolio. Many financial websites offer them for nothing, just search for 'free portfolio tool' (and only settle for one that doesn't want reams of personal data from you).

Fill in prices and dates on the tool, and then keep a brief investment diary, recording why you buy or sell each company (we'll get onto how to evaluate shares and build these reasons in a moment), and the dates you bought or sold. The 'why' is perhaps the most important element, because you can later check your expectations against emerging events. It can be helpful to read the financial press and try to get a feeling for the businesses involved. You will get to know the kind of events that move prices and by how much. Every month, make a note of your percentage return. Some shares will be far more volatile than others. Use share price graphs to put the share moves in context, both to that share's price history, to others in its sector, and to the broader market.

Yield and P/E

Two very important measurements for valuing shares soon crop up. Yield is the annual dividend divided by the share price. It is measured like the rate of interest on a savings account, so the higher it is the more income you get. However, a share dividend isn't guaranteed like the rate of interest on a savings account, and there can be huge variations year to year on what a share will pay out.

All things being equal, a high yield is better than a low one because it means more income for your capital, but there are all sorts of issues.

First, the stated yield is based on the last payout. It is backward-looking. If this year the market fears there won't be a dividend, the price falls, making the yield look temptingly high. In fact, you might not get the cash at all. So many investors prefer to look at *fast-growing* dividends. As we saw from Figure 10.1 in chapter 10, the compounded return from a rapidly increasing dividend can after a few years overtake a steadier higher income. But more broadly we can say that a long history of steady dividend increases is a pretty sure measure of a company in control of its destiny.

There are, of course, many companies that pay no dividend. Given how central dividend reinvestment is to our total returns over the long term, it is important to have a pretty clear idea why you pick a share that provides no income.

The other measure is the P/E or price–earnings ratio, a measure of how expensive a share is, and a measure we will be coming back to again and again. It compares what you get in profits per share for the money you spend. The price is there in black and white, but what about the earnings? These earnings (or profits) are essentially the pool of money the company has left after paying its bills (and from which any dividends may be paid), divided across all the shares the company has. If a share has a P/E of ten, that means you must spend 10p to get 1p of post-tax earnings per share. Another way of thinking about it is that it will take ten years of 1p earnings for that share to have 'earned' what you paid for it. Let's take a real-life example.

Marks & Spencer shares closed at 428p on 13 August 2014, according to Google. The P/E ratio was given on the same page as 13.3. We don't know from the page what the earnings per share were, but we can work it out. If it takes 13.3 years for the shares to 'earn' their price, then we can divide 428p by those years and come up with 32.18p. Simple. This is, of course, based on the last set of reported earnings.

Clearly, from this calculation, it can be seen that a company with a share priced at 78p is not necessarily more expensive than one priced at 9p, any more than a plastic bag of supermarket apples for £1.50 is necessarily more expensive than a single apple from a market stall for 30p. With apples, it all depends on the number in the bag, and the quality. With shares it depends on the earnings, and their quality too. The P/E acts like those little labels on supermarket shelves which give you the price per 100 grams. Essentially, the higher a P/E ratio, the better the market thinks the growth prospects of the company are. The reason is that when company profits are growing, it will take fewer years for a share to 'earn' its price. If a company with a 100p share made earnings of 10p in year one, then 20p, 40p and 80p in subsequent years it would have 'earned' its share purchase price in three and half years, not ten. It is also vital to look at the forward (or prospective) P/E if you can, because this measures the price against an expected future set of earnings, not one from the past.

This is just another example of the rule that the stock market always looks forward. It is expectations that drive prices, sometimes expectations years ahead. In recent years some high-technology and biotechnology shares have run P/Es of over 100. The shares would not 'earn' their purchase price for a century, so this may sound like a very long-term investment indeed – *unless* those earnings are increasing (or expected to). If the earnings are doubling every year, it would take *less than eight years*. Shares in such a firm, starting at £1 and moving up in line with earnings, would reach £64 by the end of the seventh year – here we begin to see some parallels with the story of rice grains in chapter 1!

In fact, such growth rates are rarely tenable for long. P/E ratings of this order are described by market professionals as 'highly demanding', even if earnings are keeping up. It is just like the short odds on a star horse which is assumed to win almost every race for which it is entered. The 2014 fall from grace of the online retailer ASOS Plc, whose shares halved in a few weeks even as revenues grew strongly, shows that these highly strung thoroughbred stocks are often riding for a fall. There is an old and very sensible stock-market rule of thumb which says don't buy a share whose P/E is higher than the annual growth rate in earnings. Backing known stars is fine for your phantom portfolio when you are learning the ropes, but may be a bumpy and unsuitable ride when you start using real money.

Why share prices move

The price of anything ultimately depends on supply and demand, and shares are no exception. On any ordinary trading day, some investors will buy shares and some will sell. Share prices can fall not just because there are more sellers than usual, but because of fewer buyers than usual, or a combination of the two. If a large investor sees, for example, BT shares at 370p, and decides to buy a million, then a computer will execute the order for him. Years ago in London making a trade used to entail a broker walking across the stock exchange floor to the market maker's pitch, which was a hexagonal booth. These days the market maker has in its computer lists of conditional deals, such as 'buy 1000 BT if the price falls to 366p' or 'sell 10,000 if BT rises to 380p'. Buy-and-sell deals which are *not* conditional on price (known as market orders) get matched up against each other, and then against the conditional orders. The buyer wanting a million will probably soak up all the market sell orders, so the market maker then looks for conditional sales at say 372p. There may be 25,000 in total for sale at that price, a long way short of a million. So the price marches steadily up as the big order is gradually filled.

These are the mechanics of how daily supply and demand determines share prices, but there are also shifts in the overall balance of supply and demand. If a company is partially state-owned, like the banks RBS and Lloyds, then news that the government is going to offload more of its shares on the market will depress prices. Similarly, if one company buys another using new shares in itself rather than cash to pay the owners, the share price is likely to fall because the extra supply of shares will one day find their way back onto the market. However, when a company decides to list its shares on an overseas stock exchange, perhaps the New York Stock Exchange or Tokyo, then by opening itself up to a new set of investors it is creating additional demand, and the share price often rises. Incidentally, the overseas closing prices for UK companies are very useful pointers for London market makers who set the corresponding starting prices for those firms in sterling here each trading day.

Priced in expectations

Share prices move all over the place, but quite often movements after news for the company follow a particular theme. There's an old stock market saying, 'Buy on the rumour, sell on the fact', which quite well describes the behaviour of some short-term traders. Let us say that XYZ Plc reported a 50% rise in pre-tax profits and a 20% higher dividend. Surprisingly, often the shares fall on the day, despite the apparently good news. Usually, it is about performance relative to expectations. Let us suppose that XYZ was expected to produce a 60% rise in pre-tax profits and a 30% dividend increase. The shares may have been rising in the days before the news in anticipation of this. In that context, a fall on the day might well be rational. Those who bought when they heard the rumour, and sold for a profit on the day it was confirmed (thus pushing the price down) would certainly agree. This is how the market works.

It works just as well the other way round. A company that reports disastrous results, stopping the dividend and sacking staff, might well find its share price rising on the day, particularly if the news was expected to be even worse. Once again, share prices are adjusting to expectations.

A very common form of price movement is one we can call contagion. One company reports disappointing results, and the share prices of rivals in the same industry get hit too. Much can depend on the reason. If it was a brewer saying that summer takings were hit by poor weather, then it is not unreasonable for all brewers to slip a little, but if the reason the brewer gave for the disappointment was an interruption in supply because of brewery maintenance then it should be less contagious. Technology companies are particularly vulnerable to contagion for two reasons. One is that not many investors really understand what they do (and in the absence of real information, rumours are all the more powerful). The second is that their value is often dependent on meeting demanding targets well into the future.

One other principle illustrated here is the nature of market information. Much of the time, share prices move first and only later is there any explanation of why. A share rises, then next day a big pension fund announces it has taken a 5% stake in the firm. A share falls, next week the chief executive discloses he has sold half of his stake in the firm. Even takeover bids, which are governed by very strict rules on disclosure, are frequently preceded by price rises in the target company; not always, but a surprisingly large number of times. Sometimes there is good reason, perhaps directors of the two firms were seen dining together, but more usually not. The stock market is a huge rumour mill, and those rumours move prices.

A final determinant of share-price movements is market mood. This is examined in detail in chapter 14 because of its importance, but suffice it to say the cycles of bull and bear markets, and fashions in particular sectors, can distort prices for months or even years.

It is important to emphasise here that for the purposes of multiplying your money, most daily share-price movements can be ignored. What we are after is long-term growth, and that is the trend you can see on a share price chart measured in years, not hours or days. That long-term trend is driven by one thing, and one thing only: the profit performance of the underlying business. Nevertheless, we still need to understand why prices fluctuate, because we need to know when we can confidently ignore them and when they may start to matter. Just like tuning in a radio, there comes a point when through the static you start to hear the tune, perhaps faintly at first but recognisable.

Economic theory says that prices in large marketplaces such as a stock exchange are always rational. A share price invisibly embodies all the knowledge about a particular company at a given time, akin to the mysterious movements of a ouija on which thousands of hands are resting. The trouble with this view is that it equates knowledge with pricing power. An investor who reads a share tip in a newspaper about a firm he has never heard of before and buys 10,000 shares has more effect on its price than a veteran employee of the firm who can see the business going downhill and is selling 100 shares.

In practice, we know that shares are mispriced much of the time. The market is a moody, fashion-conscious, panicky beast given to mania and depression, sensitive to rumour and gossip. For knowledgeable investors, this is the joy of the market. Every so often it presents us with fantastic bargains that we can buy, or offers ludicrously high prices for what we already own. We really can multiply our money, if only we have the knowledge and confidence to take advantage of these moments.

Where to get information about companies

A lot of books on finance tell you that to buy shares in a company you have to get your nose deep into the balance sheet, work out the value of net assets and generally spend weeks turning yourself into an unpaid investment analyst.

This is nonsense. However, it would be foolish to pick up a Sunday newspaper, read a tip for a stock you have never heard of before and immediately decide to buy it without doing some wider research.

Most of the largest public companies in the country, those that are members of the FTSE 100 share index, are written about frequently in the press and online, and during your months of phantom portfolio monitoring you should collect the more pertinent articles on the stocks you are following. Look for the company's website and its investor relations section, which will have a lot of information you'll want. You can add to this easily by your experience as a consumer. Most of us visit the supermarket, buy clothes, use a bank, consume electricity and use mobile phones. Are you impressed by the products or service? Does Vodafone customer service answer your queries more rapidly than that of Orange? Does Marks & Spencer have better products than Matalan? Asking a few casual questions of the sales assistant in PC World can give you an insight into consumer trends: are iPads or smartphones the present of choice this Christmas?

When you have narrowed down the stocks that interest you, you can download the companies' annual reports, or at least skim through recent results statements on RNS, the regulatory news service. Are earnings per share growing? Are sales up every year? Is there a chart showing a five-year earnings record? What is the breakdown in sales and profits between businesses? How much debt have the firms? That is all history, of course, and what you are really buying is the *future* of these companies. Skim through the self-congratulatory blurb from the chief executive, and find the section that talks about future prospects. It is often quite short, and frequently seems vague, although in fact more time will have been spent on it than any other part of the text. If you read a results press release from a company based in the US or which has listed its shares there, you will find a cautionary statement. This gloomy statement lists everything that could go wrong with the business, essentially in case a shareholder ever decides to sue the firm for misrepresenting its prospects. The issues it raises are ones for all shareholders to consider.

Those prepared to spend a little money can usefully subscribe to *Investors Chronicle*. Though I must declare an interest as a former contributor, the *IC* is still the easiest way for UK investors to find out what makes companies tick.

The internet is an invaluable tool for company research, often providing for free the kind of information that a few years ago was only available to professionals for hundreds of pounds a month.

That doesn't mean to say you have to be glued to your computer for hours every evening. That really isn't necessary. An hour or two a week may well be enough. In fact, the problem may turn out to be stopping yourself spending too much time looking over your investments, which can lead to unnecessary tinkering and overtrading. Keeping a balance is important.

There are several websites which freely provide analysts' estimates of major companies' earnings. Look up the companies you are interested in and download the figures.

Other useful types of information are records of directors' share dealings in their own companies. Never mind what they say, if board members are buying shares in their own companies, they really are putting their money where their mouth is. Heavy and continuous buying by one or more directors is always a good sign, although small purchases by a newly appointed director may just be an act of politeness, particularly in some US companies where it is policy for all directors to have a stake in the firm. Sales by directors are more complex, and cannot automatically be construed as a sign of worse times to come. Directors need, like anyone else, to spread their investment risk and it is sensible for them not to have all their money tied up in the company that employs them. The times when directors can sell are heavily constrained, not just by the mechanics of option agreements, but by stock-exchange rules on insider trading. Nevertheless, if a chief executive sells all his shares in the company he runs, investors will inevitably draw conclusions.

The *FT* carries a table of recent director dealings every Saturday, and numerous websites also report them. Getting professional investment analysis for free is possible now, through several websites, although nothing I have seen compares to the quality and depth available on US stocks.

Your research will allow you to gradually winnow out unsuitable companies until you have a handful of first-class businesses. You are looking for a consistent upward trend in profits and sales, strong management, some measure of market power (so they can raise prices if they have to), a position among the biggest three in each of their important marketplaces, and a business you can understand.

Never buy shares in a business you don't understand. Don't be shy about it: some businesses are immensely complex. No less a man than Warren Buffett, a self-made billionaire and one of the most successful investors of all time, claims rarely if ever to have owned a high-technology share. He maintains that he finds it impossible to understand and therefore accurately value the businesses involved. Knowing your own limitations is a good way to avoid trouble – just ask Buffett.

There is as great and subtle an art in picking stocks as there is in picking a partner for life. The most glamorous may leave you in debt after a short and expensive fling, while the outwardly ordinary may flower magnificently. Hundreds of books have been written about it, because it is one of the most engaging topics in the field of investing. It is covered in detail in chapter 13.

Choosing a broker

When you have been tracking your phantom shares for a couple of months, you might feel ready to spend some of your real money. Before you have decided what to buy, you need to find a broker. There are two basic types: the traditional advisory brokers which will charge you perhaps £35–50 per deal, depending on size, but which offer you all sorts of investment advice, or the execution-only brokers which can charge as little as £5, but do not offer advice. A half per cent in stamp duty is levied on any share purchase, so for a £2,000 purchase this would cost £10. Some advisory brokers set minimum investment levels for new accounts, and in a few cases these can be tens of thousands of pounds.

Most brokers offer either a telephone call centre or an internet dealing page, or both. Beginners often find it more reassuring to get a telephone dealer to guide them through the process, though it is likely to cost you more. The first question you will be asked is whether you want to deal 'at the market' or to set a limit. Essentially, a limit means you will not pay more than your stipulated price for the share, which might mean you can't buy it at all if the price moves above your limit. This ensures you don't pay more than you had expected to. Buying at the market means at the best price the broker can manage. A telephone dealer will always tell you the current price, and most dealing pages do so too, although prices can easily move by the time the deal is executed.

Dealing with 'the spread'

Once you make your first deal you will also discover the spread, the two different prices quoted depending on whether you want to buy or sell. Don't bother to learn what 'bid' and 'offer' mean. All you need to remember is that the worse of the two prices from your perspective is the one you will deal at. The gap between them is where the market maker makes his income. On some thinly traded shares, and on some bonds, this spread can be quite wide. One pitfall to avoid: if you put in an order out of market hours, or over the weekend, it will be executed in the first few minutes of trade the next morning, when spreads typically tend to be extremely wide. Avoid setting 'at the market' orders that will be executed at these times, because you pay more to buy and get less from selling.

When you have given your instruction, write down any deal reference number quoted to you, the name of the phone dealer, and the time. On rare occasions when there is a mistake or a dispute about what was said the brokerage will need to refer to its phone recordings, and having this information will save a lot of time. Similarly, if dealing by internet, keep the email receipt, and make a note of any error codes if there are problems making the deal.

Deals set at a limit price cannot, of course, be confirmed until they are triggered. Check when the limit expires. Most internet-based brokers allow you to set limits for weeks or months as well as hours. When you add up all the costs, you can see that frequent dealing in small numbers of shares in small, thinly-traded companies is a sure-fire way to lose money. That is one reason why it makes sense to invest for the long term. It's less work, it's cheaper and it makes you more money.

Don't put all your eggs in one basket

It's obvious really, but if you put all your money in a single company then your entire wealth will ride on just a few crucial assumptions about that one company's growth and prospects. Whatever its actual progress, the inevitable gyrations of market rumour alone can make you queasy, just like sitting in a tiny dinghy in choppy weather will pitch you from one wave to another. But if you are in a cruise liner, whose hull is simultaneously riding on thousands of waves, you barely feel a thing in most kinds of weather. The same approach to investment can smooth out the voyage too, and that is what building a share portfolio is all about. You may not be able to do it at the start, but by the time you have £10,000 invested you should be able to spread it over three or four different shares, with some cash too. More than that can make individual holdings expensive in terms of dealing and management fees.

A portfolio is not just a collection of shares, it is a structure of several investment ideas, combined to minimise the risk to your capital. Imagine it like a chair, each leg being an idea. Would you sit on a chair with one leg? Three is pretty solid, and four is great. At the end of 1999 one investment idea might have been 'The internet is going to change the way we do business out of all recognition, and I want a part of it'. If that was the only leg on your portfolio, you were pretty sure to be sitting on the ground by 2001.

But if you had three other ideas to share your investment weight across you would probably do better long term. Perhaps you wrote down in your investment notebook that 'Construction companies are pretty cheap, paying good dividends and growing steadily', plus 'We all seem to be living longer and getting wealthier, so prescription drugs might be a good bet', and finally 'This volatile market makes me nervous. I'm keeping some money in cash'.

If you take this top-down approach you can think through your expectations. List all the things that could go wrong with any of your ideas. What would happen in a recession? What if interest rates rise? Is inflation about to rip away?

Most of these economic risks are big enough that you can see them coming and adjust your position, but there are plenty of others that can crop up quite quickly. Profit warnings can hit any stock, and bankruptcies and insolvencies can flash up out of nowhere. Even if the bad news does not affect your shares directly, the market backwash can. When it does, a year's gains can evaporate in a few minutes.

Even as a beginner, you can do better. Don't commit to a single strategy. Strange as it may seem, your portfolio is safest when the ideas pull in different directions. Pharmaceuticals or food producers may look pedestrian when the economy is booming, but if suddenly interest rates are whacked up to head off an inflationary crisis, you will be glad to have them. Similarly, chip design companies, mobile phone manufacturers and all sorts of volatile high-technology companies may be out of favour when the economy is turning down but if you never own anything in that department you are going to miss out on some of the most dynamic risers when the economy picks up.

Like sitting on a chair that has just lost a leg, balance is everything.

The ingredients of a balanced portfolio

The cautious investor will spread a share portfolio across cyclical, defensive and growth companies, with some resources held in cash. The relative weightings will vary depending on the state of the market cycle.

A **cyclical share** is one in a company that does well during economic booms but badly during recessions. Although most companies have some cyclical elements to them, some firms – and their share prices – are slaves to economic cycles. Examples include steelmakers, airlines, car manufacturers, fashion retailers, holiday companies and many technology firms. We will deal with technology companies in some detail in chapter 13, because they are some of the trickiest investments, but suffice it to say now that very few are insensitive to economic cycles. Some, such as microchip manufacturers, are extraordinarily cyclical (although to a cycle all of their own), while basic computer support firms tend to be less so. As a rule of thumb, the more futuristic the products of a technology firm, the less well it will ride out a recession. Many never make it round a whole economic cycle.

Defensive companies are those whose businesses are relatively immune to business cycles, and whose share prices tend to be less volatile as a result. Pharmaceutical firms, particularly the larger ones, are classic defensive companies. The thinking goes that people fall ill whatever the state of the economy, and will continue to need medicines. People also need to eat and drink, which is why food retailers, food manufacturers and brewers tend to be considered defensive. Those who smoke do so come hell or high water, so tobacco stocks are another classic defensive play. The other significant defensive stocks are utilities, including water or electricity providers. Their businesses may not grow much in boom times, the thinking goes, but they don't shrink either, and they often pay fat dividends.

Growth companies are those which manage a pretty consistent rise in profits year after year, which is of course something we would like to see in all our investments. Looking for reliable growth at an affordable price is worth a whole book in itself, although I have only devoted half a dozen pages to this, in chapter 13. The best of the pharmaceutical firms are true growth stocks, as are an elite grouping of technology firms, but you can find growth firms hiding in other places too. The trouble with growth stocks is the hundreds of impostors, priced just as richly as the real things.

Cash is clearly a flexible addition to any portfolio. The higher share prices seem to be, the greater the amount of cash in any cautious investor's portfolio. It stops you losing money at the market peak, and it prepares you for bargains in the trough.

Pigeon-holing companies isn't easy anymore. You may have bought shares in a brewer thinking it defensive, only to find that it actually made more money from hotels (which are cyclical). While you are thinking what to do about it, your company then sells its brewing interests to concentrate on hotels. Similarly, many so-called defensive utilities, tired of labouring under a strict UK regulatory regime, have branched out abroad into all sorts of businesses, and the vagaries of their success can either double overall profits or halve them. Not very defensive, then.

In truth, most shares represent a mixture of businesses, some defensive, some growth, some cyclical, and because of the evolutionary nature of companies they will continue to change after you have bought them. That isn't necessarily a problem, so long as you can understand what you own. After all, the managers of such companies are trying to do the same as you are – to build a portfolio of businesses that will grow reliably. A balanced company helps build a balanced portfolio.

It is important to draw the difference in risk between sentiment and fundamentals. Sentiment is the ocean swell, to continue our metaphor, representing the overall volatility and cyclical nature of the market you are investing in. This is a fairly well-documented phenomenon with known, though – at the very top and bottom of the cycle – somewhat elastic boundaries. Market cycles are examined in chapter 14 and, despite the acres of newsprint devoted to them, should not cause a long-term shareholder to lose too much sleep. What you should examine is *fundamental* risk, the business performance of companies within your portfolio measured against their peers. That is where doing your research homework will save you from big and expensive mistakes.

Conclusion

- Running a paper portfolio is the safest way to learn about the markets.

- Share prices are based on forecasts of future earnings and growth.

- Price moves measure the gap between reality and those expectations.

- If you don't understand a company you will not recognise when it is over- or underpriced.

- Almost all the information you need is available for free.

- When you spend real money, don't put all of it in one share or in one industry.

- With lower commission and a huge choice of brokers, the process of buying and owning shares has never been easier.

CHAPTER 12.
Understanding Companies

"Business is like a car: it will not run by itself except downhill."

American saying

Introduction

I F WE CHOOSE SHARES TO MULTIPLY OUR MONEY, WE NEED TO BE familiar with what we have bought shares in, i.e. companies. We need to know what makes them tick, the types of event that affect them, and how they can work for us instead of the other way around. By the end of this chapter you will know:

- why investing in companies produces superior investment returns

- how to read a basic company results summary

- the events that affect companies and know how to turn them to your advantage

- why companies are driven to make acquisitions

- why so few of those deals produce long-term benefits

- what a share buyback or management buyout tells us.

In 1982 a defence electronics company called Racal was awarded Britain's first cellular telephone licence and set up a subsidiary which began to provide mobile phone services. That subsidiary company became Vodafone and its shares were floated on the stock exchange in 1988. At that time, the average mobile phone was the size of a briefcase and cost around £1,000. Now, almost everyone has a mobile phone, and the smallest can squeeze into a cigarette packet. Vodafone, through good judgement and some luck, has grown into the world's second-largest provider of mobile phone services (the largest is China Mobile). Those who were astute enough to buy the shares at the first opportunity have seen them grow in value 20-fold over those years, from a (share split-adjusted) 11p to 220p in December 2014. This is just price gain, the real gain – particularly in recent years when the price has been less perky – has come from reinvesting the dividends, and is better still. But now the company faces new challenges in an era when even Mongolian shepherds have mobile phones. Where is the growth to come from?

Buying shares in a company is quite unlike any other type of investment. A share includes a certain slice of assets, but its real long-term value is that it stakes a claim on a ferment of ideas and effort produced by a particular group of people. Unlike any other investment, companies can change out of all recognition over the course of a few years, buying new businesses, selling old ones, developing new products, changing management and staff levels, incurring or repaying debt, being taken over or split up. Companies are living, growing things while a gold bar, a consignment of cocoa beans, or a short gilt future, whatever happens to its price, will remain the same. It is this organic nature of a company, the way it grows as if through cell division, that gives the potential of multiplying your money, and is why shares outperform all other investments over the long term.

Events in the life of a company

Flotation

Lots of interesting and important things happen to companies before they reach the stock exchange, but like a debutantes' coming-out ball, the flotation (or initial public offering, IPO) is the moment that they really need to convince the world of their attractiveness. Those seeking a stock-market flotation for the first time might be young independent companies that have outgrown traditional sources of capital. They might be sales of stakes in subsidiaries, which are called spin-offs, or they might be firms like Debenhams, not only a familiar retailer, but one taken private by private equity groups then refloated.

In Britain in the 1980s and early 1990s most of the biggest flotations were sales of state-owned businesses such as British Gas and British Telecom (BT), or the wave of mutually owned building societies and life insurers converting into companies, some of which came close to collapse in the financial crisis of 2007–9.

From an investor's perspective, the crucial consideration is a basic one. When a company comes to the market, someone is selling and they are choosing the time to do it. Whether it be the original entrepreneurs offering part of their stake, or a venture capital company which has nurtured and guided the firm in its formative years, a private equity company that took the firm private, or a government that needs the money, a decision has been made by those close to the company that this is a good time for them to sell.

This makes it extremely hard for the potential investor, who must assess whether it is a good time to buy. And that comes down to the quality of the business and the price demanded. Even decent companies which come to the market at the height of a boom may turn out to be poor investments because they are priced sky high, while immature or unproven firms rushed onto the market at such times often spiral into oblivion. However, during market slumps flotations dry up because vendors cannot get the price they want, so the flotation table is not level and bargains are few.

An expensive process – which you pay for

Organising a flotation is an expensive and exacting process, involving vast amounts of time and effort by corporate financiers, tax experts and high-flying lawyers – all among the highest-paid people in the country. If you buy the shares, of course, you will be indirectly footing part of the bill. An investment bank is appointed to be the lead manager, which means coordinating the entire effort, using all its resources and contacts to drum up demand for the shares with institutional investors. If the issue is underwritten, as most are, it means groups of big investors are being paid a fee to take up any surplus shares. This is designed to stop any danger of the share price falling immediately after launch.

In fact, it is considered so important for the price to rise (creating what investment bankers call a 'good aftermarket') that the lead manager works hard to get an oversubscription, where more shares are requested than will be available. This means that applicants get only a portion of what they wanted, and investment institutions are forced to top up their holdings to an economic size by buying in the marketplace once the shares start trading. This gets the aftermarket off to a good start!

If you are considering buying shares in a flotation, you will need to contact your stockbroker (though in some cases you can register at a website of either the company or the issue's lead manager). You will be sent a prospectus which details the company and will include details of the company's last results. Quite often there is a forecast of profits and possibly a dividend for the next results. Any newly offered company should be examined just like any other investment.

Here are a few rules of thumb:

- the longer the company's track record, the safer you should feel with its forecasts and guidance

- prefer dull but concrete achievements to stellar promises

- unprofitable companies should have a clear timetable to profit; losses should get narrower, not wider

- top directors should include some with wide experience of business, not just those whose experience is of developing a single product

- avoid unproven businesses models, especially if the products being offered are also unproven

- invest in what you know; If you have read the blurb twice and still cannot understand what the company does, steer clear.

Demutualisation

Many of us have found ourselves owning shares as the result of a building society, friendly society or mutually-owned insurer turning itself into a limited company and then floating on the stock exchange. Far from being merely customers, we were delighted to discover that a building society account or with-profits life-insurance policy came with a slice of ownership too. However, most of the delight in this probably evaporated during the financial crisis when most of Britain's banks had to be rescued, including a rather large proportion of those that had been demutualised.

The damage to the mutuals hasn't ended there, either. The woes of the Co-operative Bank have consigned Britain's foremost ethical lender into ownership by a hedge fund. It all goes to show that banks, like any company, are vulnerable to hubris, complacency and excessive risk-taking.

Fortunately, barriers to entry are now coming down in banking, and along with a whole series of new conventional banks there are peer-to-peer lenders. These companies effectively act as intermediaries between investors, who supply the loans, and borrowers. P2P companies such as Zopa, Lending Circle and Ratesetter offer investors a choice of what returns they would like, usually between 5% and 8%, and then allocate their money across dozens of carefully checked borrowers willing to pay such sums.

It is important to recognise that P2P may feel like high-interest saving, but it is actually investing. The income is not only uncertain in the case of default, but taxable too. Though P2P lenders are now regulated, there is no government-sponsored safety scheme like there is for bank savings. The first P2P ISAs should arrive in the next year, allowing investors to protect their loan income from tax. This could well be a useful way to multiply your money, but I suspect that it should perhaps only take one year's worth of ISA contribution, with other ISAs used to diversify exposure.

Privatisations

Privatisations are another of yesterday's UK investment themes, another form of flotation. There is not too much left in the state's cupboard that can easily be sold, not at least to a retail shareholding audience. However, there is plenty of interest in the companies that were privatised, and to see what has happened to them underlines the unpredictable evolution of the corporate world over a decade or two.

Overall, privatisation has been a mixed bag. It is worth remembering that many privatised companies have unique franchises or assets that are almost impossible to replicate, and they continue to be regulated as private companies even as they were controlled as public ones. The obvious examples are water and power utilities, and of course BT, which has a pair of twisted copper wires going into almost every home in the country. When we talk about technological innovation, people tend to think of microchips and mobile phones, but forget the expanding possibilities of the most humdrum equipment.

Company results

We are never going to understand our investments if we don't have at least a basic idea of how well a company's businesses are doing. Company results tell us this, and they are the bread and butter of information for investors. The bald facts are there from 7am on a company's results day, on free regulatory news services online and in the financial press. There is always plenty of analysis and interpretation freely available for the largest companies.

The obvious starting point is that you should know when companies you have shares in are going to report. Most British companies report results twice a year, but there are also interim management statements and much else that may move share prices that may not even be scheduled.

Company results come in the form of a profit and loss account. Usually there is an accompanying statement too. Figure 13.1 shows a fairly simplified one for a big housebuilder called Bovis Plc for the first half of 2014.

Bovis Homes Group PLC today announces its half-year results for 2014.

Financial and operational highlights for H1 2014

	H1 2014	H1 2013	Change
Revenue	£322.1m	£184.4m	+75%
Operating profit	£51.2m	£20.5m	+150%
Operating margin	15.9%	11.1%	+4.8ppts
Profit before tax	£49.4m	£18.m	+166%
Basic earnings per share	28.8p	10.8p	+167%
Dividend per share	12.0p	4.0p	+200%
Return on capital employed*	13.4%	7.7%	+5.7ppts
Net debt	£(45.3)m	£(48.4)m	

*ROCE is EBIT for 12 months to 30 June divided by average of actual opening and closing capital employed.

Figure 13.1: Simplified results statement for Bovis Plc

The basic format starts with revenues (the money the company was paid by customers), with each line of the table then deducting a series of costs to produce a figure to compare to the previous period:

- Operating profit is the money left after most costs have been deducted, and the operating margin measures that as a percentage of revenues. Clearly the higher the margin, the more of the sales revenue is being retained.

- The next line is pre-tax profit, which is operating profit minus net interest costs on debt. This is important because profits built on borrowings may turn out to be unsustainable.

- Earnings per share (EPS) is the net (i.e. after-tax) profit divided by the number of shares in issue, and is by definition the maximum amount that could be distributed on each share.

- The dividend is that portion of EPS which will be distributed to shareholders.

- Return on capital employed is a very important number, because it measures the profit-generation of each pound used in the business. Comparing the cost of capital (i.e. debt and equity) with the returns on it shows how intrinsically profitable a business is.

- Net debt is the money owed after subtraction of cash balances and other liquid assets.

Profit warnings

"The rule is, jam to-morrow and jam yesterday, but never jam today."

Through the Looking-Glass by Lewis Carroll, 1872

A company has, according to stock exchange rules, a duty to communicate simultaneously to all shareholders any change in circumstances which may affect its shares. Naturally, this would include results that are expected to fall substantially short (or substantially exceed) consensus forecasts. Disappointing the market, with its overblown expectations and knee-jerk nervousness, is something that finance directors and investor relations specialists hate. Communicating bad news without lasting damage is as tricky a process as breaking the news to a strait-laced grandmother that your little sister is gay. Accomplished well, nudges, hints and nods lead to the appropriate conclusion. Done badly there are shrieks and tears, and possibly a heart attack.

Where the departure from expectation is not severe, the finance director or chief financial officer has traditionally spoken to those stock-market analysts whom he trusts and massages down their forecast figures. That is frowned upon these days, but still happens. Gradually, the consensus slides, and any share fall is not precipitous. Professionals particularly watch for changes in forecasts from the company's own brokerage, which often lead that consensus down.

However, where it becomes clear there is going to be a loss instead of an expected profit, or a slowdown from 90% expected growth in earnings to 25%, there is no choice but to issue a statement. The meat is often buried at the bottom of a long news release, underneath all sorts of public relations waffle about 'confidence in the long-term future of the company' and 'prompt and radical action'.

Some of the worst-handled profit warnings occur after a company delays, usually without explanation, the release of scheduled results, or slips out a brief statement on Boxing Day, Good Friday or some other time when the directors imagine nobody will notice.

How the market reacts to profit warnings depends on what stage in the mood cycle it is in. If the market is rising strongly, then even quite sizeable disappointments are overlooked, but in a bear market everyone is looking for an excuse to sell. Much also depends on how highly rated the stock was to begin with. A much admired company trading at a P/E of 100, and which has never failed to match market profit expectations, can be savaged by its first relatively minor shortfall, while a lowly rated firm that frequently disappoints the markets has much less far to drop.

Rights issues

Companies seeking extra capital often return to tap their existing shareholders through a rights issue. New shares are offered to shareholders in proportion to those they already own. The price of the new shares is rarely higher than the current share price, and quite often at a significant discount. Don't assume that because the new shares may be cheaper than the existing ones they are automatically good value. Taking up the new shares merely allows you to keep the same proportionate ownership of the company.

Almost always, shares fall on news of a rights issue, even if shareholders are fairly enthusiastic about what will be done with the money raised. It is the certainty of sharing the available profits more widely, combined with the prospect of better profits down the line. Jam tomorrow, as Lewis Carroll remarked.

If you decide not to take up your entitlement, it is important to notify your broker that you wish to sell those rights, not to let them lapse, because some shareholders will want to buy more than their entitlement. As soon as the shares become ex-rights (the first day when buying a share in the company ceases to entitle you to subscribe for new shares) there will be a market in what are called nil-paid shares. Seasoned investors sometimes sell their rights, but then buy nil-paid shares which allow relatively cheap, but more risky, exposure to the share-price moves.

Rights issues are often underwritten if there is any doubt about the demand for them. Underwriting institutional investors will, for a fee, guarantee to buy up any unwanted shares.

Placings

A placing is a private sale of shares by a company, normally to a restricted circle of investment institutions, and conducted through one or more brokers. If this is a capital-raising exercise they will be new shares, but sometimes it is done to minimise the market 'splash' when a large block of shares is sold by an existing holder. Those placings that are easily arranged without much of a price discount speak volumes about the institutional affection for the company in question.

Takeover bids

Takeovers and acquisitions are when one company buys another, normally by agreement. Many large companies are in the process of buying and selling dozens of small businesses or assets at any one time, but it is the larger deals that attract attention, especially those where the target company is unwilling to be purchased. This situation is unique to listed companies: no one can forcibly acquire a privately owned company.

The financial press loves nothing more than a juicy hostile bid, in which each company rubbishes the financial record of the other. Effectively, the battle is being fought for the hearts and minds of shareholders in the company for which the offer is made, because they decide whether or not the bid is accepted.

So what is it that gets everyone so excited about takeovers? The answer essentially is money. To buy up a public company means buying all the shares, buying out every single shareholder, the pension funds, the insurance companies, the directors, their families and trusts, and so on. The acquiring company usually has to pay quite a lot more than the target's shares are currently trading at to do this.

Takeovers are the icing on the cake of stock-market investment, so long as it is the target company that you own stock in. There are many investors who do little but scour the specialist press for takeover tips and candidates. It is not a very reliable way to make money. A takeover story is a useful addition to an investment case that is already tempting on fundamental grounds (i.e. the business is good and the price not too high), but you need to be sure that you have a sound investment in case the bid you are hoping for never materialises.

The mechanics of takeovers

For substantial takeovers, the company making the purchase usually offers new shares in itself in exchange for the shares in the target company. Shares, being the promise of profits in the future, are considered an easier payment route than cash on the nail. If cash is offered as an alternative, it will normally be on less-generous terms.

Here's a simplified example.

Blue Plc launches a bid for our company, Yellow Plc. The terms, announced first thing in the morning before the stock exchange opens, are three new Blue ordinary shares for every two shares in Yellow or a cash alternative of 131p per Yellow share. This won't get us very far until we look up the share prices of the respective companies.

As shareholders in Yellow, we already noticed that the shares yesterday jumped 20p to 137p on the rumour of a bid. Blue's shares closed yesterday at 95p, down 12p, because it was rumoured, correctly as it turned out, to be the bidder. At the close yesterday, shares in Blue were worth 95p, so three were worth 285p, which divided between two shares in Yellow is 285p ÷ 2 = 142.5p each, a whole 7.5p more than the Yellow price at the close! The cash alternative looks rather less generous, but then cash is cash, while shares fluctuate in value.

Yesterday's prices were a fairly decent stab by the market at what level any bid would be pitched, but once the market opens today it will have the actual terms to work with. Immediately we notice Yellow shares rise another 10p to 147p. But Blue shares drop another 5p to 90p, worsening the share swap terms considerably! 3 × 90p = 270p, which ÷ 2 = 135p. This is 12p adrift of the price the market puts on Yellow shares, and only 4p more than the cash alternative. What is going on? In the next day's newspapers you read that the terms were not considered generous, and other bidders may be attracted now Yellow is 'in play'.

This game can go on for some time, with manoeuvrings, negotiations, perhaps new bidders, and the chance of increased terms from the original bidder. The good thing about takeovers (if you already hold shares in a target firm) is that you have a while to mull over what to do. You can either sell your shares in the market, or wait to accept the share swap terms or take the cash alternative. If you are opposed to the takeover, you have the opportunity to vote against it, though money usually tells in the end. It rarely makes sense to be in a hurry to make your decision, because prices do tend to firm up as the takeover situation develops.

This example was an unsolicited bid. Agreed bids are usually tied up by the time the news is first released, although it doesn't stop other bidders stepping in. Mergers are those takeovers in which the two companies are of roughly equal size, particularly if the number of shares issued by the buyer gives the shareholders in the seller control of more than half the shares in the combined company. However, for public relations reasons, almost any takeover is described by those taking part as a merger.

There are thousands of ramifications to takeovers, but we can distil a few guidelines:

- shares in target companies usually rise on news of a bid

- shares of the bidder tend to fall

- consider the possibility of other bidders stepping in

- if the bid was unsolicited, consider the chance of rejection, and possibly improved terms by the bidder

- don't be in a hurry to sell a target's shares in the market

- weigh up the chances of intervention by the Competition Commission or another regulatory body: this is one occasion when selling a part of your target company holding can be wise

- if you believe the bidder is overpaying for the business you hold shares in then don't accept a share exchange: sell in the market or take the cash alternative instead

- accepting share exchange terms does not trigger a taxable capital gain

- if you sell for cash you will trigger a capital gain, except if you hold the shares in a tax-exempt wrapper, like an ISA.

Almost all takeovers are justified on the grounds that a new combined entity will be more effective than the sum of its parts. Anyone saying this should be treated with the same kind of scepticism as door-to-door salesmen and their wonder products. Academic research has repeatedly shown that the majority of takeovers fail to add value in the long term. There are a whole host of reasons for this:

- underestimating the complexities of the integration process

- overestimating the true value of the acquired firm

- overpaying to win control

- relying on the dubious arithmetic of earnings enhancement

- regulatory stipulations and delays

- loss of key management and staff

- poor due diligence.

There are huge complexities involved in putting together two large companies with different activities, different locations, different accounting and computer systems, and different management and staff cultures. The biggest promised savings come from attempts to remove 'overlap' between firms, e.g. two banks each with a branch in the same town, where only one will now be needed, unifying central functions such as purchasing or sales administration, or jointly purchasing advertising space. These can meet with staff resistance, particularly if job cuts are involved.

Quite separately, there are what are called synergies. This buzzword has come to describe the cross-pollination of two companies working together. Examples include the classic *bancassurance* model, where a bank and an insurer merge, and the bank staff use their contact with customers to sell them financial products from the insurer, or the drugs merger economies of scale where the uncertain returns of developing each individual new drug are spread over a larger number of candidate compounds, and the same salesmen sell a broader range of products.

It is not uncommon for a company that agrees to be taken over to have hidden problems or issues which stop the merger reaching its full potential, or mean that the acquirer has unwittingly paid too much. These can include overstated results, aggressive revenue recognition (counting your financial chickens before they have hatched), hidden losses or debts, overvalued stock, and so forth. Due diligence, which really means checking the paperwork over thoroughly, is the way to root out these problems.

Takeovers are expensive. There are investment banks and advisors to pay, documents by the lorry-load to print and distribute, and management distracted from running their own business. That is before the cost in shares and cash of making the purchase. The target company usually ends up being offered substantially more than the assets of the company are worth to win the approval of the target's board. That excess is called goodwill and ends up appearing on the balance sheet, where a portion of it is amortised or written off against assets every year. Considering the billions in goodwill some companies incur on over-optimistic takeovers, it is hardly surprising that covering this with extra earnings is no easy task.

Of all the many exaggerated benefits of takeovers and acquisitions, one in particular is worth examining: the 'earnings enhancing acquisition'. It means that earnings per share, taking into account all the costs and savings of the takeover, will be higher after the deal than they were before. After all, this is surely the bottom line. How can shareholder value be improved if earnings per share do not rise? Despite a million tonnes of glossy paper issued by advisors talking up synergies, critical mass, and so forth, the most important factor in earnings enhancement is actually a little magic arithmetic.

Here is a simplified example. In Table 13.1, Big Firm makes an agreed takeover of Small Firm. Big Firm has been increasing earnings at 20% a year, and is valued by the market at 20 times last year's earnings, while Small Firm increases earnings at half that rate. Its slower growth means that you can buy 10p worth of its earnings for £1, whereas you only get 5p worth of Big Firm's earnings for that price.

Now Big Firm offers to buy Small Firm in a straight share swap, one for one. Even before a single redundant office chair or filing cabinet hits the skip, Big Firm has still magically managed to enhance its

EPS by 20%. The reason is quite simple. It is swapping via the share exchange only 5p of its earnings for every 10p of Small Firm's. However, for owners of Small Firm shares, the EPS has fallen by 40%. For them, this deal is dilutive.

Table 13.1: Big firm buys small; firm earnings per share jump 20%!

	Big Firm	Small Firm	Combined
Net earnings	£1,000	£500	£1,500
Shares in issue	20,000	5,000	25,000
EPS	£0.05	£0.10	£0.06
Share price	£1	£1	£1
P/E	20	10	16.7
Market value	£20,000	£5,000	£25,000

In reality, matters are even worse. Takeovers are usually conducted at a premium to the target company's share price, which will eat into the earnings enhancement, so it is beholden to the acquirer to estimate how much money they will save. This is often made to sound very precise, but I am convinced that some companies work out how big the savings need to be to justify the takeover, and only then work out what operations at the target company will be chopped or sold.

Buyouts

A buyout means a company returns to private ownership, and is either undertaken by a private equity company or by management. Private equity companies usually substitute debt for equity, and chop costs hard to get a quick return. Some have been pilloried for selling off valuable land and property, loading companies with debt, and paying themselves quick dividends. Most private equity companies try to get the firm sold back on the stock market within two to three years.

A management buyout is a very strong signal that management believes the market is undervaluing the company, or part of the company. The timing often means the terms offered to shareholders do not seem overgenerous.

Share buybacks

Companies can either repurchase shares in the market or, less commonly, make a public tender for a proportion of their own shareholders' stock. Either way, it tends to boost the value of the remaining shares, first because earnings are now spread across fewer shares, and secondly because of the effect of a big extra buyer in the market. Companies sometimes buy back their shares to compensate for the dilutive effect of options granted to staff and management, or as a tax-efficient alternative to paying dividends. Occasionally shares that are bought back are not cancelled, but retained in the treasury department for use as an acquisition currency. A large share buyback is a strong signal of an undervalued stock price.

Bankruptcy

Bankruptcy, the winding up of an insolvent company, means that a court appoints a trustee (or receiver) to sell (liquidate) what is left of the assets for the benefit of creditors. While extremely common for small building firms or garages, it rarely occurs to large public companies. Size matters here. Remember the old adage:

> "If you owe a bank £100 and you can't pay, you're in trouble. If you owe the bank £100 million and can't pay, then the bank is in trouble."

For the major-league indebted there are a hundred exits before the buffers, and most large failing firms succeed in taking one or another. One of the most common is administration, where an externally appointed specialist manager attempts to satisfy creditors while running the business as a going concern.

This can mean radical job cuts, dismemberment and sale of parts of the company, and the closing of unprofitable lines. It frequently means extra loans dished out by creditor banks in exchange for a larger stake in the company. The important thing to remember about bankruptcy is that an ordinary shareholder is right at the back of a very long queue for any proceeds. Don't wait until you get there. A pittance in the market for your shares is better than nothing.

Conclusion

You cannot invest successfully in individual shares until you have a decent understanding of companies. But once you know what makes them tick, how they live and grow, you will be able to spot the opportunities that will multiply your money. The next chapter will get you started on applying those skills to choose the right shares.

CHAPTER 13.
Choosing the Right Shares

"What counts for most people in investing is not how much they know, but rather how realistically they define what they don't know. An investor needs to do very few things right as long as he or she avoids big mistakes."

Warren Buffett

Introduction

THIS CHAPTER SHOWS YOU HOW TO MAKE THE DYNAMISM OF companies work for you. You will learn how to:

- spot companies whose earnings will grow and grow

- learn how to use the growth double-play

- buy shares for less than you know they are really worth

- time your purchases to your maximum benefit

- mix investment strategies to balance returns

- avoid strategies that lose you money.

Investing is made up of three decisions: what to buy, when to buy it, and when to sell it. Until you have completed all three, the investment process is not complete. The quality of each of those decisions will determine your returns.

As you read through the following sections, one thing above all else will become apparent. The successful investor, the one who beats the overall market, is the one who runs against the herd. That entails buying stocks that are undiscovered, neglected, or misunderstood, which practically speaking is the only way to get them cheaply, and selling them when they become widely known, fashionable, hot and overpriced. This is known as contrarian investing, and because of the power of market psychology, no part of it is easy. The four key dangers are poor judgement, fear, greed and herd instinct.

Poor judgement, because some shares are justifiably neglected, and a cheap share that falls further is as expensive as they come. Fear, because selling a great share too soon leads to the loss of the major part of potential profits. Greed, because selling too late can cause your profits to evaporate in the few moments it takes for a market darling to issue a profits warning. Herd instinct, because if fund managers with millions of pounds have been selling a stock, it is extremely hard to believe you should be buying it (and vice versa).

We are bound to make mistakes. However, it is essential for us to avoid letting our initial mistakes turn into disasters. A regular and unemotional review of investments, particularly those that are performing poorly, is essential. Amateur investing has often been likened to amateur tennis: the game is decided by whoever makes the fewest mistakes. To improve your tennis, you work on minimising those strokes you frequently drive into the net or out of the court, not by trying to perfect an already decent top-spin lob or passing shot. To improve your investing, you cut your losses and let your profits run.

Let us start by looking at the two main techniques for choosing shares: growth investing and value investing.

Growth investing

Growth investing is the most popular investing technique, and by tradition is where the big money is made. The growth investor identifies companies that have superior products and services, that are increasing their market share, and – most importantly – have the strength of management to make that advantage last for year after year. Once certain which companies fit the bill, the growth investor buys and holds for years, sitting tight through the inevitable dips and doubts, always there for the rapid share-price recoveries and the long-term increase in earnings.

The growth investor may not be too concerned by dividends, but is aiming for consistent capital growth as the share price is driven up by the value of the underlying business. However, the best growth businesses do gradually throw off cash, and fast-growing dividends can make a good growth story great.

Growth investors know that a company's share price may deviate and wander but in the end will always return like a faithful dog to follow the course of earnings. If the earnings consistently climb, then so will the share price.

The set of growth plays comes down to:

- pure and established growth companies

- promising young growth candidates

- companies transforming into growth stocks.

For the pure growth disciple a track record of earnings growth is enough, and they buy in, whatever the price of the share. If earnings are increasing by 36% a year, they argue, then so will the share price.

In two years the shares will therefore double and whatever the price paid for the stock, it will in retrospect look like a bargain. However, there are dilemmas: proven growth is expensive, promised growth is uncertain, and cheap growth is fleeting.

The rule of thumb from chapter 9 was not to pay a higher price–earnings multiple for a company than its long-term rate of earnings growth. Yet it has been extremely difficult in recent years to find pure-growth companies at less than this multiple. In fact, you often have to pay a premium over it for those companies that produce growth year in, year out. The only way to get established growth plays cheaply seems to be to wait for those moments of disappointment or market doubt over the durability of growth. If you get to know the company well enough you may identify those moments (and they can be just a few hours) when a nervous market has overreacted to some small piece of bad news. The universal rejoinder from those who examine these stellar pure growth stocks, is "I wish I got in at the start, when it was cheap."

Smaller growth companies

Let's try looking for tomorrow's growth stocks while they are still minnows instead of paying over the odds for today's whales. There is some academic evidence that small growth companies as a group have returned better share performance than larger firms. However, they are much harder to research than big firms (both because less is written about them and they put out less about themselves), they generally have short track records, and they are expensive to trade in terms of spread and volatile in their share-price movements.

For those who are prepared to do the groundwork, and particularly those with an accounting bent, there are rewards to be had. When a small company is recognised as producing superior growth, it can soar at an astonishing speed. However, one precaution is essential. Spreading your investments among small companies is even more vital than with large ones because when market sentiment turns against a small firm, or if it disappoints profit expectations, there may be no second chance. The fall is just as rapid as the rise, but more permanent.

Finally, there are plenty of investment books out there by very successful professional investors which advocate getting to know small companies before the brokers and tipsters, finding nuggets of information known to no one outside the company. It can be done, but rarely by amateurs, and is increasingly hard even for professionals these days. After all, what company is going to give management time and a tour of the factory to someone who only has £5,000 to invest?

False prophets of growth

Some of the best growth stocks have started from nothing and then virtually created the industry they grew to dominate over a decade or more. The most widely cited example is Microsoft, in which many investors who got in near the start in the early 1980s would have seen their investment multiplied 100-fold. Many millionaires were created, not just directors, but because of the widespread use of stock options as a form of pay, secretaries, programmers, and administrators too.

However, it has to be said that for every firm like Microsoft (or Apple) with the power to consistently increase profits for 15 or 20 years, there are hundreds of others which grow strongly for a few years and then fade, and literally thousands that seem to promise rapid growth but never deliver it. If we are taking this bottom-up approach, how can we tell them apart at the outset, before we have the track record of earnings to examine?

Many investment books try to make looking for growth into a rigorous science. Only pick the top two companies in any marketplace, they might say. Or look for an industry with barriers to entry so that competitors cannot easily get in. Strong business franchises, e.g. a road builder that owns the only quarry near an area of major construction, or the operator of a sole airport in a particular city, have their fans too. Certainly these are starting points for the search, but in truth they are never the whole story. Finding growth stocks is like finding good friends; they emerge gradually from those you know and spend time with. You can't sit and stare at a list of characteristics and infallibly pick them out.

Many things emerge over time. Anyone can see now how useful mobile phones are, but in the early 1980s, when they weighed as much as anvils, they never really looked like becoming mass-market products. What everyone was excited about then was Bio-Isolates, a British firm that had developed a long shelf-life substitute for egg in cakes, and an American firm called Nimslo which invented a camera that took 3D pictures. I've no idea what happened to those firms, but acres of newsprint were devoted to them at the time, and many thousands of people invested in them. Even when the right industries were spotted, such as home computing, the early pioneers like Sir Clive Sinclair and his ZX Spectrum did not turn out to be the long-term winners.

It all seems very easy in hindsight, but then investing is particularly prone to that kind of 'I knew it all along' mentality. In truth, it can be very hard indeed to tell which companies will make it and which ones won't. If it was easy, no one would need to write books about it.

Then there is the issue of growth life cycles. Almost as soon as most firms are crowned as true growth companies with six or seven years' consistent profit increases, they may have their best years behind them. Almost no company can for perpetuity produce above-average earnings, for the same reasons that an investment fund cannot forever produce better-than-average market returns. High returns in any industry attract competitors, while natural monopolies usually fall under regulatory scrutiny. Business franchises are eroded, brands age, and technologies change. When pure growth stocks become cheap, it is often because most investors believe the growth is no longer there. If you disagree and jump in you may either make a fortune or lose one. There is no escaping the investor's dilemma: proven growth is expensive, promised growth is uncertain, cheap growth is fleeting.

Technology shares

Technology companies are the most tempting but the most dangerous kind of growth play, and the smaller and more immature they are the trickier they get. These firms' products are often exciting to investors in inverse relationship to how much they are actually understood.

The more arcane the product, the less resistance there is to the hype that goes with them. As a telecommunications reporter for Reuters in New York in the mid-1990s, I was receiving two-dozen calls a day from the PR agencies of small technology companies that were desperate to get Wall Street attention. These companies wanted to draw investors' attention and lift their stock prices so they could raise more money or go on an acquisition spree. In this atmosphere there was a bidding war of words: every company was going to change the world with its product or service. They felt if they didn't make grandiose claims they would be ignored by reporters, and they were frequently correct. It is much easier to make outrageous claims about a new product when it is a box of microchips than when it is a box of chocolates.

Choosing the right shares

Be sceptical. Only a tiny fraction of technology companies will prosper in the long term. Like mayflies many have only a short time to establish themselves, get their product known and understood, and make profits before the next wave of new ideas overtakes them.

Quite often they never get as far as the profit part, and the founding brains depart for pastures new, leaving shareholders with a big stake in yesterday's ideas. History shows us that the best technical products rarely triumph, but the best-managed and the best-marketed usually do. Bill Gates may look like a computer programmer, but he didn't write MS-DOS, the software operating system on which Microsoft's fortune was built. He bought it cheaply from another company, which I think is the ultimate piece of contrarian investing.[15]

A lot of this is about who you are, and how much work you want to put in. Employees in information technology may well be able to keep up with the shifting sands of who's top in their industry. A National Health Service employee might be better advised looking to growth stocks in biotechnology or healthcare. Retired people may want to settle for calmer waters altogether.

If you invest in technology stocks, there are big profits to be made, but your time horizon will have to be shorter, your investing nimble and your research extensive. Finally, remember that technology investing is safest, like all investing, when it is out of fashion.

The growth double-play

A growth stock is one that shows growth in the earnings from the business, irrespective of what the share price is doing. However, there are techniques that allow you to take advantage of both growing earnings *and* the way the market values those earnings.

Let us say you bought shares for 100p each in an engineering company, which last year produced earnings of 10p per share (a price–earnings ratio of ten) and had a history of increasing its earnings by 10% a year. However, this year, one of the firm's new products is very successful, and earnings rise to 12.5p, a growth of 25%. That lifts the

---

15   Author Robert X. Cringely in his book *Accidental Empires* says Gates paid $50,000 for the rights to an operating system written by Tim Paterson at Seattle Computer Products and then made a deal to provide it to IBM. I wonder how Paterson feels now.

shares by 25% to 125p (still a P/E of ten), but after a second year of 25% growth the market realises this is not a dull engineering firm but an exciting growth company, and should be valued at a P/E ratio of 25, in line with its new earnings growth rate. So what happens to the share price by the end of that second year?

The second year's earnings are up 25%, so 12.5p × 125% = 15.6p, then × 25 (for the P/E ratio) results in a share price of 390p.

Bingo, 390p! We have nearly quadrupled our money in two years. It is tempting to hang on for further gains at this point, but we must be wary about the quality of those gains in case the market has now gone from underrating the company to overrating it. Once the double-play has taken effect, the chances are that we have seen the steepest climb in value of the investment. So if we have any doubts about the sustainability of the new earnings growth, we should pocket our winnings, tip our hats at management, and say goodbye.

The flipside of a growth double-play is that it can operate in reverse, and the consequent fall in the share price is usually even more rapid than its earlier rise. Many savvy investors scour companies looking for transforming growth double-plays, but this is one area of growth investing in which the inexperienced stand a reasonable chance.

When researching companies, it is essential to focus on the earnings and business prospects, understanding what makes each company tick, irrespective of what a share price is doing. Do not rely on favourable newspaper coverage, however universal it seems to be, as a substitute for researching a business; indeed, it is much more likely to indicate a good time to sell than a good time to buy. Share tipsters and newspaper reportage are drawn to share-price rises like moths to a candle. As an investor you should check your growth stocks regularly to make sure the share price is not getting too far ahead of the actual earnings growth. If the P/E ratio consistently expands then it is only the hot air of promises and expectations that is filling the gap, and you are unlikely to regret selling at least a portion of your holdings.

Choosing growth stocks comes down to feeling your way gradually:

- spend time evaluating the candidates

- choose moments of market weakness to buy into proven growth

- be sceptical of growth candidates; spread your investments

- look for the growth businesses hiding in a dull stock

- always look for opportunities for the growth double-play

- be prepared to sell part of your holding if the P/E moves too far ahead of earnings growth.

Momentum Investing

Momentum investing means buying shares purely because they are already rising, in the expectation that still more investors will clamber aboard the gravy train. Unfortunately, it has a superficial and dangerous appeal to those new to investing, because it seems to offer quick and easy profits with little or no research. But like an exhilarating ride on a runaway train, there comes a moment when you realise that the driver, the guard and the ticket collector – everyone who really understands what drives this investment vehicle – have quietly jumped off, and now it is heading at breakneck speed into the buffers. In short, do not buy shares purely because they have risen, unless you know the chart techniques of how to spot failing momentum, which is the trigger to sell.

Value investing

Value investing is a good place for any inexperienced investor to start. It appeals to those who enjoy poking around in discount stores, buying 20 J-cloths for 50p or a dozen thick garden bin bags for £1.

To spot a stock market bargain you must have done your homework beforehand. Value investing in its purest form takes advantage of the fluctuations in market pricing which sometimes make a company's share price less than what we know we would get if we sold its assets and paid off its debts. This net asset value accords no value to the business itself. If the company is paying a good dividend, as such lowly rated companies often are, that can be an extra attraction.

Quite often the underpricing of assets is to do with land. Many companies which are struggling in their businesses are sitting on a goldmine of development land. The real value of the land may not be immediately apparent if there has not been a revaluation recently, but if the price of the stock is less than the net assets per share (a figure you can get from the annual report) it may be worth a closer look.

There are other types of asset too, even if it is harder to put an exact price on them. In consumer markets, a long-established high-street presence and a trusted brand name are assets with real value. Some brands are easy to value. If a tin of Heinz baked beans costs 6p more than a supermarket's own brand, then that is what the consumer will pay for a product embodying trust and familiarity. To profit from this, Heinz just has to make sure that establishing and maintaining this brand through advertising and so forth costs a lot less than 6p per tin.

So you can see that sometimes there is a kind of bargain-basement value beneath which a share price should not fall, even if the business is doing badly. Assets become more valuable the harder they are to replicate, and the harder the business is to enter. Unique values are similarly attached to assets such as broadcast rights for Premier League football, the rights to publish Harry Potter novels or land in the city of Macau, which is the only place in China to allow casinos.

Emerging markets

Emerging markets in the developing world have a plausible attraction. These are dozens of emerging markets around the globe which have been tempting western investors in recent years. There is no standard definition of an emerging market, but they do tend to share certain characteristics. These can include:

- moving from a planned to a market economy

- low but fast-growing disposable income

- less stable political and financial institutions

- weak business, market and environmental regulation

- opening up to international capital and trade barriers

- immature stock markets.

Why would you buy into emerging markets?

This is where the economic growth is fastest, so it is entirely reasonable to suppose that the companies that operate there will produce faster profit-growth too. The BRIC countries, Brazil, Russia, India and China, were all the rage for several years after Goldman Sachs economist Jim O'Neill coined the term in 2001. But funnily enough, right from the start Russia was a dangerous flop for most investors (just ask BP) and Brazil and India soon disappointed. Only China has remained an investor obsession.

For investors there are only two key ingredients in emerging markets. One is the promise of higher returns than might be obtained at home, and the second is the benefit to a portfolio of spreading risk.

The problem has been that in a globalised world emerging markets are increasingly linked to western economies. Emerging markets may not all be affected together, but they do reflect the economic cycles we see in the west, sometimes in exaggerated fashion. In the past decade emerging markets as a whole have failed not only to outperform most western markets, but also to offset the risk of western markets. They rose when western markets rose, but by less, and fell with them too, except more. The rest of the time they wriggled and rolled to their own rhythm,[16] a volatility which even in the good times was seen as their biggest disadvantage.

For most investors their advantages are overplayed. To see why, you have to see what underpinned their attractions in the first place. Once emerging markets have fully emerged they will have acquired the characteristics of western economies, both good and bad: a more reliable banking system, but lower economic growth; better financial disclosure, but more regulation; and a better educated but more costly workforce.

Many of the benefits of emergence are one-off events: privatisations, permission for local pension funds to buy into privatised assets, freeing of international capital movements, and permission for foreign investors to acquire local companies. Above all, the main benefit was their discovery by western investors. Once these processes have run their course, that is it. You then risk being left with investments in an economy you understand less well than your own, which is growing no more quickly over the course of the business cycle, and which is much more volatile. On top of that, the costs of accessing those markets are higher, even though with the rise of specialist ETFs they are lower than they used to be.

Besides, there are other ways to harness the power of emerging markets. Many well-known British and American companies make much of their money in emerging markets, from the fashion houses that rely on Chinese purchases of handbags and shoes to tobacco firms like Imperial and banks like Standard Chartered and HSBC.

---

16   Over a longer period, the MSCI Emerging Markets index has risen around 9% a year since 1987, against 5% for UK shares but with much greater volatility (*Investors Chronicle*, 25 July 2014).

They used to have a saying on the New York Stock Exchange: "If a stock is less-attractive than IBM, then you might as well own IBM." The same is true of investing abroad. If you are going to take the trouble to invest abroad, why not choose the economy that has been emerging for 150 years? In many ways the US has all the advantages of an emerging market. Throughout its history it has sucked in cheap labour from all over the world, provided land and education in abundance, and let them get on with it with a minimum of regulation. For investment returns it is a hard formula to beat.

Avoiding mistakes

Advocates of particular investment strategies often make their name by claiming dramatic success for those that follow their techniques, whether it be investing in junk bonds or distressed securities, or buying the biggest-yielding stocks in the Dow Jones Industrial Average. For a while the herd theory guarantees that some pundits will attract sufficient followers for it to appear to work, just like pyramid savings scams which promise astonishing rates of return seem to work at the start. But like outperforming funds, the returns on any easy-to-replicate technique will always revert to the mean once it becomes widely followed, and for the same reasons. The securities in question become expensive. The market is a peculiar machine, in that its performance is governed by the feedback of expectations.

Anything that promises market returns well above average should be treated with the greatest scepticism, particularly by the inexperienced. If you can't understand how the returns are generated, then you may be being hoodwinked. If you can, then the scheme is sure to be rapidly copied. The inexperienced investor should aim for solid rather than spectacular returns. Beating the market is more likely to come about from rigorous attention to eliminating poor investment decisions and cutting costs, than by adopting fashionable techniques.

The seasoned investor is an agnostic, making growth, value and cyclical investments where they seem appropriate, but rarely all of one type.

Conclusion

- Pick a balance in your portfolio between growth and value investing.

- Avoid stocks that are so highly priced they can only disappoint.

- Look for transforming growth double-plays.

- Look for growth lurking within dull, underpriced companies.

- Look for hard-to-replicate business assets or market position.

- Pounce on pure growth stocks in brief moments when they are cheap.

- Don't expect to get it right every time.

- Keeping trimming your costs.

CHAPTER 14.
Mania and Depression: Profiting from Market Moods

*"If you can keep your head when all about you
Are losing theirs and blaming it on you"*

If by Rudyard Kipling, 1910

Introduction

EVERYONE WHO OWNS A HOME KNOWS ABOUT THE CYCLE OF markets. Sometimes house prices charge up 15 or even 20% a year for six or seven years, and then perhaps they fall 5 or 10% for a couple of years. Those who buy at the top sometimes get caught in dreaded negative equity, where the loan on the house is worth more than the house, but overall, in the long term, the market moves up in its wiggling, S-shaped way. If you first got on the housing ladder during a recession when everyone was afraid of losing their job, you may well have got a bargain.

Replicate this in the stock market and you will make money above and beyond the average rise in the market. Buying when everyone else is selling and selling when everyone is buying is called contrarian investing, and done properly is an excellent way to boost your returns. Those who have been investing since 2000, when stock market returns have been more muted, may doubt this, but when the stock market breaks above its 1999 high – which it eventually will – you will regret not having participated.

Pound cost averaging

You can reap the benefits of contrarian behaviour even without directly owning a share, so long as you invest regularly. Let us say you spend £100 per month contributing to a market tracking unit trust with varying prices around the year, so that the number of units purchased also varies (table 14.1).

Although the average price at which units were available throughout the year was £1 exactly, the variation in price has worked to your advantage, getting you an extra 31 units, and cutting your average cost per unit to 97.5p, a 2.5% saving. This effect, known as pound cost averaging, is extra performance that will be compounded year in, year out, as we saw in chapter 2.

Table 14.1: Pound cost averaging

Contribution months	Price of units	Monthly inv.	Units bought
Jan–Mar	£1.20	£100	250
Apr–June	£0.80	£100	375
July–Sept	£0.90	£100	333
Oct–Dec	£1.10	£100	273
Year	£1	£1200	1231

This level of price volatility is perhaps big for one year, but the process works just as well over three or four years. A 30–40% dip once every five years can do wonders in bringing down the average cost of units bought. Of course, you can do even better if you decide actively to take advantage of price variations, which is where contrarian investing really gets to work.

Investment seasons

Investment runs curiously like farming, in that there are seasons to sow and seasons to reap. History shows that there are certain times when investors gain a little bit of extra tailwind in their investment performance by buying or selling just ahead of the crowd. You don't have to conform to these, but it is essential to be aware of them.

US investment newspaper *Barrons* reported a study into the old adage 'Sell in May and go away'. It found that investors who bought stocks in the S&P 500 index on the first trading day in October and sold in the following May every year would have grown a $10,000 initial stake in 1950 into $600,000 by 2000. Those who bought in May and sold in October would have turned it into only $13,000, which is a pretty astonishing difference. The comparable figures for the UK are equally amazing. The late stock market historian David Schwartz calculated back over many decades that the UK stock market has risen by an average of 13% from November to April in any year, but by less than 1% from May to October.

Some of the reasons are obvious enough. The summer is a season of low activity because of holidays, while the start of the calendar year is a time of new beginnings, financial and otherwise. Ever since the start of personal equity plans in the 1980s, and their ISA successors, the end of the tax year on 5 April has brought a last-minute rush of investment by those hurrying to use up their tax-free allowances before they expire.

But October, for no concrete reason I know of, has a massively disproportionate share of sharp market falls going all the way back to 1929. Contrarian behaviour therefore tells us to invest in the depths of an October sell-off, or shortly afterwards, and be there for the January buying boom (which in most years has moved backwards right through December as everyone tries to get in early) and use the strength of the market in early April as a platform from which to ditch unwanted shares. I'm not advocating ditching your entire portfolio every year – that would hugely raise transaction costs – but to pick your moments to add fresh money and realise profits. Of course, individual years may vary enormously, but on average it doesn't seem a good idea to buy in September or to sell during an October sell-off. Leaving your ISA shopping until the last minute (or doing it in the first minutes of the new tax year) also looks to be a losing plan.

Investment institutions have their own seasons that contribute to market activity, with books to be squared at the end of each quarter (known as window dressing) and new money to be spent at the start. In the US, the last few sessions of the year (US tax and calendar years sensibly coincide) make up what is known as the tax-selling season, in which the stocks that were hammered worst during the year take a few final blows as investment funds bail out. The losses made are then set against taxable gains from profitable stocks.

Buying low and selling high is extremely hard to achieve consistently, because markets never move in precisely the smooth, predictable way you want. While market bottoms are often reasonably easy to spot, tops can be tricky.

Market moods

To make money investing you need to get a feeling for the strange and irrational beast that the stock market is.

Boom-and-bust stories occur again and again, with only a slight twist. In the late 1960s it was a group of stocks called the Nifty Fifty, in the 1980s it was the turn of biotechnology and microcomputers, around the millennium it was the turn of the dotcom stocks, perhaps the biggest bubble of all. Now it is biotechnology again, and smartphone app start-ups. In ten years' time it will be something else.

Hype and depression are part of the cycle of the market, whether it is for the market as a whole, as in the crashes of 1929 and 1987, or for just one sector, like technology stocks in 2000–01. They are an opportunity for the sceptical investor, because they lead to mispricing, and the less well-understood a company or sector, the greater that mispricing will be. This means that if you do understand a company or sector, and can keep your head, you can make a lot more money during these phases of the market.

Circles within circles, wheels within wheels

We are now going to time travel through a complete and fictitious stock-market cycle, from bust to boom and back again. Normally a trip that takes several years, we are going to compress it into a few pages.

The hangover

We start immediately after a big market collapse. It is the sort of time when small investors, bruised by their recent experiences, never want to see another share again. When the Sunday papers arrive they flick straight to the sports section or the colour supplement. The business and personal finance sections are never opened; it is all too painful to think about. What money was left at the broker's has been dragged back into a savings account. Suddenly, from nowhere, long-forgotten investment categories begin to be publicised, like preference shares, permanent income bonds and so on, which offer dull but predictable returns, a promise of dry land for the seasick investor. Long-term growth funds are ditched as investors recall last year's broken promises. Many switch their ISAs to bond funds.

On the markets themselves, a few of the bigger firms are quietly picking up in value although many of the smaller stocks remain mired near all-time lows. In the weekend section of the *Financial Times*, directors of a few hard-hit companies are noticed to have bought stock in their companies. Nevertheless, the paper's Lex column sternly warns investors that they should wait for firm evidence of improved profits before committing cash to the market. Interest-rate cuts may be sufficient to stop any further declines, it says, but prices are still not overwhelmingly attractive.

Return of the headache

Indeed, the industrial news does get worse. Profit warnings are borne out, and companies warn that there are no signs of recovery. A few old established businesses in engineering or steel throw in the towel after a 20-year decline. Job cuts come by the thousand.

The CBI and unions wail about the destruction of the manufacturing base, and, sure enough, interest rates are cut again. (The Bank of England acts like a man whose shower has suddenly gone cold. He clicks up the economic heat but nothing happens. Shivering under a freezing stream, he cannot wait, so he keeps turning the dial. When the hot water arrives it is comfortable for only a moment and soon starts to scald.)

The stock market has begun to recover. The more adventurous professionals have been buying like crazy, and some funds are starting to boast of their 'bottom-picking' skills. Overall, however, volume remains a fraction of that in the boom and small investors fear that this will be just another of those suckers' rallies they got caught in before.

This is the time that experienced investors start to move back into stocks they know well. Prices may make a final downwards jerk, but for the long-term holder it will not be significant. Acting now can lay the foundations for spectacular gains.

Six months go by and the market is well above the lows. Some of the highly-rated technology and biotechnology stocks with three-digit P/E ratios are 20 or 30% above their lows. The defensive utilities, drug companies and tobacco stocks are having trouble making headway as investors who parked their money there during the crash now find more exciting prospects.

Financial advisors remain cautious. They recommend staying in government bonds or cash until the situation clarifies.

The aspirin take effect

It is a year or two on from the crash and investors have begun to forget the pain. The broad market rose 30% in its first 12 months, even more in the case of some of the volatile technology shares. Oliver Lemming, a neighbour, throws his *Daily Telegraph* down in disgust. "ABC e-commerce has recovered to 275p," he says. "That's twice the price I sold it at in the crash. Wish I'd held on to the damn thing now".

"Ah," you reply. "But it is still less than the 940p you told me you bought it at. Do you think it is a bargain?"

"I don't know," he says. "I never did understand e-commerce."

In the second year, prices rise another 20%. Cautious investors feel they may have missed the boat. Venture capital firms have no such qualms. They are investing in thrusting young entrepreneurs and new ideas, which will come to the boil just in time for the next boom.

Old ideas re-emerge in new guises. Focusing on core competencies is out, conglomeration (usually with some new-fangled name) is back, or perhaps vice versa. Takeovers begin to be seen again, mostly agreed but with the occasional hostile bid. Investment banks are taking on staff again. You start to hear about even fatter year-end bonuses for 21-year-old traders.

Share prices make the occasional attempt to go lower, but each time buyers step in at the lows. A channel of rising prices remains intact.

Hair of the dog

After months of indecision, an aged aunt who has pestered you about what to do with her building society windfall finally takes action of her own. She has read in the newspaper about the emerging market in Korea and let a clean-cut young salesman persuade her into putting her £10,000 into the Acme Korea Special Situations fund. "He was ever so nice, and I get a free pen and travel wallet," she says. "But what are special situations?"

Optimism spills out in all directions. The newspapers are full of the new crops of companies coming to market. One has discovered a marvellous new drug which cures cancer in mice, and might do so in humans once they have raised $200 million to cover the cost of clinical trials. Another company, founded by a teenager, allows social media users to send each other a thumbs up sign, and already has 550 million users. Sponsors predict Facebook will pay $2 billion for it.

Investors begin to feel that perhaps it isn't too late to buy, seeing as the market hasn't fallen so far.

Markets in places such as Brazil and Nigeria have outperformed those in the rest of the world since the crash. Funds which specialise in those areas now have sufficient cash for a big marketing push. New emerging market funds are set up, and bring in floods of new money from small investors.

Heady exuberance

It is three or four years since the crash and memories are short. Investment guru Ivor Billion, after three years of 50% investment returns, announces that he has devised a foolproof way to beat the markets every year. Books are written with titles like *FTSE 100: 20,000 by 2020*. Papers are published which seem to show that the boom-and-bust cycle has finally been broken, or that inflation will never return. This time it is different, they say. There now seems no risk to investing everything in equities. Bonds are for wimps. Many stocks make new highs and trading volumes become huge. The economy is growing rapidly. Interest rates may have started to creep up, but no one is worried.

Zeco Software, a company with no revenues, comes to market and the shares quadruple on its first day of trading. Phoenix Concepts, a company making a wristwatch that gives you access to the internet, makes a profit warning. It announces that it will not now break even for six years, rather than the two promised.

"This is actually great news," says one analyst. "The extra investment they are making will ensure 90% dominance of the market rather than 60%. We reiterate our buy recommendation." The shares rise by 10%.

The final binge

*"It is the bright day that brings forth the adder;
and that craves wary walking"*

Julius Caesar by William Shakespeare, 1599

Some shares in the market are rising by 10 or 15% a day. Brian Nerdly, who works in the computer department at work, boasts to you that his shares in a small Israeli firm that makes smartphone apps have quadrupled in the last year. When you ask whether it is time to sell he scoffs, "Why would I sell? This is just the start. This is the next Apple."

Investment banks are ditching all their usual rules, to hurry fledgling companies to market before the wave breaks. There is no end to the ingenuity of the market in manufacturing investments from nothing when there are investors out there who are desperate to buy. Some of these flotations are little more than sharp suits and hot air. Many of the executives have no track record and the companies have no product or revenues. Investors clamour for them anyway and there is even a waiting list to be an underwriter.

Fulton Fish Plc, a declining company whose shares are worth only pennies, announces it is changing its name to Whizzo Gaming to reflect its new (but tiny) business buying and selling stakes in online video gaming software firms.

The shares treble overnight.

The last of the famous value fund managers, who refused to pay over the odds for investments just because stocks were rising, quits. His clients are deserting him after years of underperformance. The last bear is leaving the party, only the bulls remain behind.

Experienced investors know the warning signs quite well. The saying goes that when taxi drivers start giving investment tips instead of asking for them, it is time for everyone else to get out. Clearly, when a stock market has soared so much that you are not just reading about it on the business pages, but seeing it on the main BBC news, and reading about it in *Cosmopolitan* or *Loaded* magazine, then almost everyone who is going to buy shares has done so. There is practically no one left to sell to.

By this time, seasoned investors will be taking profits. They know that when the wave actually crests there may be no time to act.

When you look at a chart of a major market index like the FTSE 100 or the Nasdaq 100, the final few days of a market top often look appropriately like a crown, perched on top of a head and shoulders. This crown will have a series of rapid upward spikes and retracements, and may well be slipping to the right as each successive attempt at a new peak fails.

The start of dizziness

During the next few weeks there is likely to be a series of vicious downward chops, with equally rapid but smaller rebounds, each petering out at a lower level. The rebounds are often caused by frustrated buyers, who either sold out too early on the way up, or missed out altogether, trying to get in at what looks like a temporary low. They can also be caused by 'short' sellers closing out their positions.

Nevertheless, the mood remains good. "It's okay," say the brokers. "Every market has to pause for breath. You can't go up in a straight line". Some of the leading companies with good market positions do actually make new highs, but selling among secondary issues brings the main indices down.

Other news events may also become associated with a sharp fall, some more logically than others. In August 1990 there was Iraq's invasion of Kuwait, in October 1929 it was a banking crisis. In the US in October 1957 it was Russia's launch of Sputnik; in the UK in 1987 there was a huge storm in the small hours of Friday 16 October, which preceded what became known as Black Monday. Then of course there was the banking crisis of 2007–8 which triggered a near halving of the FTSE 100 by early 2009.

The slide begins

Professionals are selling in droves, but the public is still heavily in the market. Some have sold, only to be tempted back in when the market begins to bounce from lower levels. It is not obvious where exactly the top may be; that only becomes absolutely clear months after the event. There is a sensible saying: "Always leave the last 10% to the next man", which is attributed to Lord Rothschild, though which one I don't know.

You hear on the grapevine that Brain Nerdly is sitting on big losses in his Israeli high-tech firm. There has been no bad news, and he's still convinced it is the next Apple. Tracy in accounts has heard he is getting a loan to buy more stock.

Against a background of peaking prices, you will probably not regret taking some profits in any stock that runs to a three-digit P/E ratio, however fond of it you are. Of course, if you are sitting on losses in such a company, you might at this point consider selling altogether.

Defensive stocks such as pharmaceuticals and food manufacturers are beginning to perk up at this point. They can make a superior parking place for cash during the early part of market falls because they often go up and pay good dividends. However, if the market later degenerates into a full-blown crash of 1929 proportions they may be hit as hard as everything else.

Slumping

Profit warnings start to arrive thick and fast, and the effects are profound. Once, when the market was soaring, even quite bad news was swept aside. Now even the shares of a company that beats market profit expectations, but narrowly, can fall. Those that miss by a wide margin come in for a fearful hammering. Investment houses that three years ago urged investors to buy ABC e-commerce at 940p are suggesting they sell, even though the price is now less than 100p.

Investors shelter, like soldiers in trenches, watching the creeping artillery barrage of profit warnings heading towards their positions, destroying every share price it meets. Some sell, others just sit tight, praying they won't get hit.

There are more days of big losses, and fewer and shorter rebounds. The few buyers out there are getting progressively more scared that they will be caught by the next big fall, and they flit in and out of the market in hours rather than days. Unit trusts find big redemption calls, which they meet by pulling back into cash. The flow of flotations dries up almost entirely. The new glamour stocks, hyped so hard on the way up, are being crushed. The word 'biotechnology' in a company name, a halo during the boom, has slipped to become a noose. Short-sellers, hunting in packs, track them down and sell, without even stopping to check what the companies actually do.

Even now, after big losses it can be wise to ditch those dubious stocks rather than hang on in the hope of getting back to break-even. It is rather like a fire at a hotel. The guests who stay longest to gather up their precious belongings are the ones who end up losing not just their shirt but their eyebrows too.

Markets overcorrect in both directions, but particularly rapidly on the downside. Those investors who bought on margin face ruin, their stocks worth less than their borrowings. Brokers close the loss-making positions for them, frequently at the worst price of the day.

Doomsters may not quite convince us that no one is going to buy soup or ice cream ever again, but they are well on the way to persuading us that every growth stock is now a dud, that the market for computers or mobile phones is saturated for good. The more difficult to understand the sector is, the more panicky the market gets about its prospects, a mirror image of the euphoria seen on the way up.

Final collapse

In the final few days or weeks, selling broadens well beyond the most highly-priced glamour stocks to embrace pharmaceuticals, tobacco firms and even low-rated utilities. There is no hiding place but cash, and that is where the money goes.

Perceptions of firms' long-term growth prospects and solid management skills count for nothing: when you are convinced the boat is sinking, grandma's antique furniture is thrown overboard along with the coal.

Some stocks can lose a year's gains in a single day, and even the most experienced of investors begin to question their skills and judgement. If you are not frightened now, then you are indeed made of stern stuff. They say the darkest hour is just before dawn, and this is it. But as long as you have husbanded some cash, you can get some once-in-a-decade bargains. It is an extremely hard principle to follow, but the more prices have fallen, the happier long-term investors should be. The darkness soon lifts, and the only way is up.

So we have come full circle, from bust to boom and back again. When prices are plunging it is as hard to imagine them soaring as it is to look out into your rain-lashed garden in February and imagine that by July you will be sunbathing there. Yet the seasons of the stock market are as immutable as those of nature.

Investors need scepticism, independence of thought and a long-term perspective to avoid being seduced by the herd mentality. Just as gossip only really travels in the absence of facts, knowledge is a great protection against market hysteria.

The better you know the companies you have invested in, the safer you will feel when the market falls. Just as importantly, your knowledge should lead you to sell when shares become overpriced.

The role of information and commentators

It is a strange truth that information in markets almost always trails price changes, not the other way round. Comments from analysts and dealers are usually post-hoc rationalisations of what has happened, because the actual truth is often unclear until sometime afterwards.

When share prices are rising sharply, analysts often nudge their profit expectations and share-price targets upwards to keep them in line with the new 'reality'. Similarly, when a share has fallen sharply they reduce them. The herd mentality thunders through the quiet, wood-panelled meeting rooms of top brokerages just as rapidly as in the sweaty crush of a market pit. Of course, the analysis is so professionally dressed up that the only whiff of the herd's passing is that shares rated a 'buy' a month ago at 900p are now an 'avoid' at 325p. It doesn't help much to have the second piece of advice if you have already taken the first.

Pass the parcel, stock-market style

The stock-market party always has the same children. There are the snooty private equity guys and their nerdish entrepreneur friends, the strange institutional family – pension funds and insurers mainly – plus those tough professional kids from next door with the scraped knees, and finally you, the investing public, who arrive when things are already well underway.

You notice that the entrepreneurs have just passed a parcel of investments quietly to private equity and venture capitalists. The institutional family comes next when the shares come to market, then the professionals and then the investing public. Each time the music stops, whoever holds the investment parcel takes off a layer of profits, then passes it on. Those that arrive late, with the hubbub and excitement at their greatest, receive less and less of a parcel. Most frequently it is just when the investing public gets to play that the parcel is finished. Unlike the real party game, there are often no toys inside, just unfulfilled promises.

The interplay of the various groups that hold shares is crucial to understanding the way the market operates. Entrepreneurs work for years scraping together the cash to build their businesses, but if they happen to be in an area that is deemed 'hot' (and contrary to what we read in the press, only a tiny minority of new businesses are) the venture capitalists, those who buy stakes in immature businesses, come knocking on their doors. The venture capitalists usually want to nurture businesses to the point that they are ready for flotation, which can also give them the chance to sell all or part of their stake at a premium. That is when the institutions and professionals come aboard, and the first chance for the investing public too. The stock may move unspectacularly for years, until it catches the crest of some wave. At this point, the investing public's appetite is whetted, and the shares may become fashionable. By the time this happens, the excitement is at its greatest and the last couple of layers of wrapping are ready to be torn off. That is a very good time indeed to pass the parcel to someone else.

Conclusion

- Think independently.

- Identify the stage of the market cycle you are in.

- Prepare for the next move.

- Never believe things are going to be different this time.

- Be sceptical.

I'm sure Rudyard Kipling had his sights set higher than a tawdry knowledge of financial markets when he wrote 'If' in 1910, but his words are nevertheless as good a creed as contrarian investors could wish for:

> "If you can meet with triumph and disaster and treat those two impostors just the same ... Then yours is the Earth and everything that's in it."

CHAPTER 15.

The Neglected Art of Selling Gracefully

Introduction

S ELLING IS THE LAST PART OF THE INVESTMENT PROCESS, AND however well we manage the first two parts – what to buy and when – if we get the last part dramatically wrong, our gains will either diminish or disappear.

After all, 'paper profits', however spectacular, only become real when they are safely cashed in. Taking profits gracefully is only one aspect of the selling skill, however. Cutting losses on failed investments is the other, and probably even more important. Failure to cut losses quickly and then clinging to investments that lose money are the two most common investing mistakes. Almost everybody makes them occasionally, but some investors make them repeatedly and are doomed to perform poorly.

It doesn't have to be that way, if we approach selling in the same methodical and disciplined way that we buy.

In this chapter we learn:

- the importance of running profits and cutting losses
- how to allow profits to push out losses from your portfolio
- when to step off the gravy train
- how to top-slice profits
- how to run with the investment seasons
- how to take advantage of temporary price spikes
- how to recognise a failing investment
- why you should reappraise a falling share before investing again
- run your profits and cut your losses.

Don't knock clichés, especially in investment. Someone is trying to tell you something. 'Run your profits and cut your losses' is an old piece of advice, but still worth a few percentage points a year in portfolio performance. It is based on the concept of 'market overshoot'. Share prices overshoot on the way up, and on the way down too. A pretty good growth stock will go from being under-appreciated, to highly rated, then overvalued and eventually absurdly expensive. Similarly, once a stock falls out of favour and selling gathers pace, it may pass into the area of being cheap and straight out again until finally it is being given away for a fraction of its net asset value.

Of these two stock valuation rides (from the sublime price to the ridiculous), you only want to take one – up. So jump off the falling stocks quickly and stay on the rising ones. The effects on a portfolio from running profits alone can be profound, and draw on the same magic of compound growth that we covered in chapter 1. If your investments are split equally between two shares, one growing by 50% and one by 10%, the high-growth share will be 60% of the portfolio in one year, then 66% the year after. As it goes up, so does the average growth rate of the portfolio, from 30% to 33% to 37% in the third year, and it continues to accelerate.

Now assume a slightly different scenario. The second share is not growing by 10% a year, but falling by 50%. After the first year the growth share is 75% of the portfolio, and after three years it is 97.5%. The losing share has almost entirely disappeared, and the growth rate of the portfolio is almost 50%.

So we can see that, left to their own devices, consistent profits push out consistent losses in a portfolio.

Stepping off the gravy train (before it hits the buffers)

In practice, you cannot run profits forever. There comes a time when you become convinced that the best is over for a particular share. It is extremely hard to generalise on this one. You cannot say it will be so many months or so many years. It all depends on the share. Sometimes you may have held on to a stock for years and gained just 20–30%, while in the froth of a boom a share may treble in six months without losing momentum. So when should you sell?

The first point of reference should be the price–earnings (P/E) ratio. Are earnings growing fast enough to justify the P/E ratio? It isn't just the price side of the equation that matters: you must be sure the earnings predicted are achievable. If a company in the same industry has made a profit warning recently, that should ring alarm bells. If you understand your investment well you will know which firms can truly be compared with yours. If the P/E is in line and the industry is booming (or your company is demonstrably winning market share), then you should generally be happy with your holding.

However, some ratings are too rarefied to be supportable beyond the formative years of a company's life. A P/E of 400, even if the firm is for the moment quadrupling profits, is incredibly demanding. A share that keeps up to this rating will quadruple your money in a year, but for some a doubling in six months would be quite sufficient.

It can be very hard to judge the right moment to exit, and it requires planning and discipline. What I usually do is set myself a 12-month price target for a stock when I buy, which I note in my investment diary alongside my reasons for buying. The point about the target is not to be accurate (I'm not notably successful) but to calibrate how your expectations change. If you surpass your expectations within six months you have to decide whether you are undervaluing the stock or the market is overvaluing it.

When a company continues to appreciate beyond all reasonable fundamental levels, true contrarians want to know who has yet to buy the shares. Once articles about the company and its directors move beyond the usual borders of the financial press, into the tabloids and magazines, then almost everyone who could invest has probably done so, and the shares usually have little further to go.

The death of the blue chip

Running profits forever would be easy if we could be sure that the prices would continue to rise year in, year out. There was a time when investors believed that some shares you just never needed to sell. They could be relied upon to produce decent growth and income year after year. In recent decades in Britain, Marks & Spencer, BT, Tesco and GlaxoSmithKline have worn this mantle. In the US there has been Apple, AT&T, Coca-Cola, Pfizer, General Electric and Microsoft. The US term 'widows and orphans stocks' said it all. These were investments that required no maintenance, and offered no risk for the long-term holder, however innocent and inexpert.

Unfortunately, the world has become rather more cruel to widows and orphans in the past ten years, and blue chips, as such companies were also known (named after the highest-denomination poker chip), are an endangered breed. Of all the companies listed above, there is not one that hasn't faced huge challenges. The nearest one to pristine, Coca-Cola, is now facing a dietary backlash against sugar, the main ingredient in its drinks. I expect its story will gradually become more like that of tobacco. Marketing alone cannot prevail.

Techniques for graceful profit taking

Once you have decided a share you own is overvalued you need to pick your moment to sell. Don't be at all shy about selling while the price is still rising. You may get more than you expect for your holding, while if you wait until there is some weakness the price may already have fallen substantially. In true contrarian fashion it can be just when all the news is excellent that there is nothing left to wait for. News of the entry of a fast-growing company into an index such as the FTSE 250 or FTSE 100 is a frequently used selling platform. Having ridden the shares all the way up, some investors simply wait for the big index-tracking funds to step into the market. These deep-pocketed funds *have* to buy, whatever the price, because they must reflect the index they are tracking – and while the price leaps because of this, the seasoned investors sell.

Selling does not have to be an all-or-nothing event. If you are unsure how much further a share has to run, you might sell a third of your holdings now, the next third in a month, and the final third in two months. This is known as top-slicing. Rather than use time, you could of course set price targets for each slice: increases of say 50%, 100% and 200%. This approach can be used by anyone, however inexperienced, and can work very well.

Whatever method you use, it is vital that you stick to it. If you put off selling because you keep revising your expected profits upwards, it could be that you are beginning to fall for the market hype. If that happens, the chances are that you will be caught holding a stock when its price collapses.

Cutting losses

Bad investments have a way of dragging us down with them. Like drugs or booze they start as a small habit, a 10% loss perhaps, and we give it some slack, waiting for a recovery to confirm our original wisdom in buying the stock, but no, the price slips again and soon we are down 30%. This could be more serious money. To sell now is to turn a paper loss into a real one, and we want to avoid that at all costs. So we turn the exercise on its head, and throw in fresh money, reducing the break-even price so the losses in percentage terms are lower (but the amount of money lost is actually unchanged). Now our cool head has gone completely and we identify so much with the stock that we get angry when it is criticised, as if it were a friend.

Instead of admitting we were wrong, we are tempted to buy still more shares as the price slides, without taking the vital step of re-evaluating the basic investment thesis. I know some investors who have done this three or more times, like an addict rationalising each successive fall and reinvestment as a greater bargain. Soon there is so much 'lost money' at stake that we can't bear to sell at all. This pretty much reverses the good-drives-out-bad principle we established on running profits. Any portfolio in which money is being poured into losers is in trouble. Either the money is fresh cash that should be searching out winners, or the proceeds of sales of winners that we should still be holding.

When you are tempted to put in fresh money to a losing investment, the first thing to do is nothing at all. Wait for it to stop falling. If a share is falling out of favour, remember overshooting; you may well have a much longer and cheaper opportunity to get back in than at first appears. Next, research it all over again from the ground up. Forget that it is a familiar company; try to think of it as a new one. Would you buy another company with those fundamentals? Are the profits intact? Only when it meets all your criteria should you go ahead and put in fresh money. Very few candidate companies should make it.

The easiest way to stop throwing good money after bad, like giving up smoking, is before you get hooked. Setting a stop-loss when any share falls say 10–15% helps avoid this. This is easily done in any internet brokerage account.

By being strict we may say goodbye to the occasional solid investment that would recover, but will miss all the dogs. Alternatively, we can pick a crucial chart support point below the purchase price and sell if a share falls through it. (Clearly, however we set sell limits, it pays to leave enough leeway for day-to-day price fluctuations.)

Recognising a failing investment

It always helps to know why a share is falling. The better you understand the companies you invest in, the more rapidly you can make a decision and the more confident you will feel about it. In essence, the more specific to your investment the reason for the share-price fall, the more reason to sell, and quickly. The most common start is a profit warning. Here is how Nicola Horlick, a well-known fund manager, deals with losses:

> "I always sell on the first profit warning. There will be optimists out there thinking there is time for things to pick up, and so there will always be a two-way trade of stocks at that point. Wait till the third downgrade and you have no hope of getting out."

Profit warnings often come in packs of three or four. It is rare for management to be able to turn a deteriorating situation around rapidly enough to avoid further disappointments, and the restructuring turnaround is often years in the making. A 20–30% loss may look bad at this point, but worse is often to come. Selling into even minor rallies after warning number one is rarely regretted. The bringing in of fresh management is often a rallying point, especially when the new chief can clear out every speck of bad news and blame it on the previous incumbent, but as Warren Buffett has pointed out, when a respected manager is brought into a poorly performing company, it is most frequently the company whose reputation remains unchanged.

Sometimes there seems to be nothing whatever wrong with a company – no profit warning, no management changes – yet its shares keep slipping. This would be the time to dig deeper, search the internet, phone the company, find out more. Usually an explanation will emerge. If not, what you should do next hinges on your level of confidence in the company. Sometimes selling half the holding before the shares slip far will soothe anxieties. I have found this a very useful technique when it is not possible to quickly find out why a stock is falling. I have rarely regretted it.

Frequently a whole sector will fall together, on worries about sales or margins in the industry. Sometimes this is justified, other times not. If your company is not actually affected, it may be chance to get a bargain buy. At other times it should serve as a warning. If every company in the industry is going to be ratcheting down expectations one at a time, there could be a drip, drip of Chinese water torture during which the shares will be incapable of rallying.

When whole markets are falling, we have a different problem: not so much bad investments as bad timing. It is good to sell early, even though it is not initially apparent how far the market could fall. By the time this is clear, it looks too late to sell. The worst thing would be to sell out at or close to a bottom in the market. That is a classic small investor's mistake. It is hard to avoid feeling anxious at these times because it is often hard to know where the bottom will be, but in fact there is less cause for worry when everybody's shares are falling than when yours alone are. See chapter 14 on market cycles for more details.

Tax: the silver lining to the loss cloud

Taxes are as kind to losses as they are unkind to gains. If you have lost money on an investment, chapter 18 lists ways of at least making something from your misfortune.

The sin of anchoring

When we buy a share, the price we paid becomes of great psychological significance, because from it we measure our gains or losses. It is a kind of Plimsoll line, with 'expensive' written above and 'cheap' written below. But we have seen before the fallacy of pricing shares on their nominal value. If a share halves in price after a shock announcement of profits falling by three-quarters, that stock is now twice as expensive, not twice as cheap. You stand to get only half what you were expecting by the only measure that really counts: expected future earnings per share.

Frequently, when a share is slipping we promise ourselves that we will not err again, just let this awful stock get back to its starting point and we can sell, say goodbye like good friends, none the worse for the nightmarish encounter. The trouble with this view is that our starting point has no significance whatsoever for the market. While the market has its own repeated tidal rhythm, the stocks within it come and go. Like driftwood, some get washed up for good. If you own a stock that has halved and halved again, it is almost certainly never going to return to its peaks, for several reasons.

First, only firms with a high P/E ratio and relatively low asset value fall that far. Secondly, a return to its former glory would mean two doublings of the stock price, a far more difficult mathematical feat than the two halvings. Thirdly, the psychological shock of the fall lands the company with a has-been label, and nothing repels the market more than yesterday's leftovers. Finally, such a precipitous fall damages a company's standing among customers and potential lenders (including shareholders and bondholders), who wonder whether it will still be around in a year's time.

And if a plunging share *does* recover and get back up to where you bought it, there must be some powerful reasons for overcoming those hurdles. There would be no more reason to sell then, when profit finally hoves into view, than for a jockey whose horse had fought its way up from the back of the field to ease up the moment he takes the lead.

The sin of overtrading

Once we have successfully completed the trading process a few times, from share selection to timing the purchase and sale, it is easy to become over-confident. The temptation is to shorten our investment horizon, imagining that we can predict and ride the market climbs and get out before the falls, profiting from the market's every twist and turn. Academic studies pour cold water on this, pointing to investors' consistent overestimation of the average returns they can achieve and underestimation of the real damage that commissions from frequent trading do to portfolio performance. A study from the University of California even shows a sex bias to this. Male investors on average trade 45% more frequently than women, and produce 1% worse performance.[17] So the message is keep your eyes on the far horizon and benefit from long-term growth, while saving enormously on both commission and time.

Conclusion

Selling is an art, not a science. Very few of us will always sell at the right time, but if we look time and again at the strength of the businesses we own, we will get the pointers we need. Sell profitable

---

17   *Boys will be Boys*: Brad Barber and Terrance Odean.

investments too early and we can miss the best of the rise, sell too late and we are in an unseemly scramble to rescue even a portion of our former winnings. For those which disappoint, sell immediately. Don't consider throwing in more money unless you are absolutely certain the market is wrong. Even then, wait for it to do its worst before you buy. You will probably get a better bargain.

CHAPTER 16.
The Employee Shareholder

Introduction

THERE ARE CURRENTLY FOUR TYPES OF GOVERNMENT-APPROVED employee share scheme and one 'status':

1. enterprise management incentives (EMI)

2. approved company share option plan (CSOP)

3. save-as-you-earn share-option scheme (SAYE)

4. share incentive plan (SIP)

5. employee shareholder status (ESS).

The details of each vary, and can be found online. If you are being offered one of these schemes, you will be given the details of how they work. This chapter is to show how to make the best use of them, and to raise awareness of some of the risks. From the employee perspective, share options are generally a great thing, although there are still several important principles to consider:

- where options are an extra to a fair salary there is no disadvantage

- the choice is harder when options are offered in lieu of extra salary, or as in the case of ESS, for reduced statutory employment rights

- consider the concentration of risk in having your employment income and savings tied up with a single firm

- once your options are turned into shares, your risk profile and tax liability increases

- you need to plan for the taxes on option gains.

Many of us first get the opportunity to acquire shares as a result of an employee share scheme. Schemes like CSOP and SAYE offer an opportunity for ordinary people to create large (sometimes extremely large) lump sums from relatively modest payments with no risk at all. It is probably the most effortless way to multiply your money because it gives you the benefit of deciding today whether you want to buy something at prices last seen years ago.

EMI

Enterprise management incentives are designed for new small firms that want to attract, reward and retain skilled staff. Firms can grant options over shares up to a value of £250,000 per employee. Implementing a plan does not require formal HMRC approval in advance. Like most such schemes there is no income tax or national insurance payable on the value of the options so long as they are granted at no discount to the prevailing share price, but capital gains tax is levied on proceeds from any increase in the value of the shares at disposal (unless, of course, the canny employee puts them in a SIPP or ISA). Shares not sold for at least a year after the option was granted get a reduced CGT rate of 10% rather than the typical 18%.

CSOP

Under CSOP, a company can grant each chosen employee options over shares worth up to £30,000 at their full price (contrast with SAYE). The options vest after 3–7 years, and if the shares have risen above the exercise price, the employee gets the gain free of income tax but is liable for CGT.

The CSOP, though not common at the time of writing, is used by companies which wish to offer participation to all employees including part-timers and those on low wages who would find it difficult to use some of their salary to actually buy company shares. Employees can use an advantageous loan arrangement to fund the purchase of the shares under option if they cannot afford them, and repay through the proceeds. This is a cashless exercise.

SAYE

The SAYE scheme is a savings scheme of three, five or seven years for all employees at an enterprise, at the end of which the employee has an option to buy shares in the employer, usually at a 20% discount to the price prevailing at the start of the scheme.

Monthly savings, contributed from net pay, can be anything between £5 and £250 a month, and are boosted by a tax-free interest payment (which usually compares favourably with savings accounts). The marvellous thing about starting an SAYE is that you cannot lose. If the share price plummets below the option exercise price, you just wait until maturity, decline the opportunity to take up your share entitlement, and merely benefit from a good savings scheme. If it's touch and go on maturity day, you have six months to wait for the share price to recover before your option lapses.

SIP

The share incentive plan (SIP) comes in four types – free shares, partnership shares, matching shares and dividend shares. Companies choose which they offer. Under free shares, companies can give up to £3,000 of shares to each employee every year. Under partnership shares employees can buy up to £1,500 of shares from their pre-tax salary each year. For each partnership share the employee buys, the company may give an additional two free shares using the matching shares module. Dividends from past years can be used to buy additional shares each year. All share types must be held in a trust for 3–5 years before they are transferred into the employee's ownership, free of income tax and national insurance. However, as the employee has ownership of the shares from the beginning, but cannot sell until they mature in the trust, there is more risk involved than in many of the other schemes. That may be a high price to pay for the tax exemption.

ESS

Employee shareholder status, introduced in September 2013, is a government wheeze, which can be combined with some of the schemes listed above, to grant certain tax advantages to employee shareholders. These include up to £50,000 worth of CGT exemption. The downside is that it comes at the cost of inferior employment rights, specifically the lack of statutory redundancy pay and most unfair dismissal criteria. It only applies where employees have been given shares, rather than paid for them.

Making the most of the schemes

So far, so good. The complexities only really arise when your company's share price is not doing so well.

Let's use SAYE as an example. Most SAYE schemes run on a rolling annual basis, so if the share price slides year-on-year you may have the opportunity to switch to a scheme just starting, which will be cheaper. However, if you switch out of an SAYE before expiry you miss out on the better part of the interest which comes as a lump sum, and you will have to go back to year one. For these two reasons, the nearer SAYE maturity you are, the bigger the drop in the price of the next option needed to justify switching. Note that if you are making less than the maximum monthly contribution, a fall in the share price is less of a problem. You merely contribute to the next scheme too, up to your overall maximum of £250 a month.

The biggest disadvantage to an SAYE, or indeed any share scheme, is that they are 'golden handcuffs', keeping you at your employer perhaps longer than you might wish. Except in compulsory redundancy, leaving a company means cancelling your SAYE with your contributions and only modest interest returned. There are only two things to say on this. First, don't decline to start an SAYE because you assume you will not be in the same job for five years, as we often stay in jobs for years longer than we expect. If you do leave, you will still get your cash back. Secondly, yes, this is a personal finance book, but don't multiply your misery by staying with a job you hate just for the options.

For some, tax is the biggest bugbear. The sales of shares acquired through an SAYE are liable for capital gains tax, just like any shares. However, some employers make it possible to contribute employee shares from SAYE or SIP into a registered pension using a SIPP. They can also be sold and repurchased into an ISA at maturity.

There are various other kinds of options schemes, with shares granted or paid for, which are not covered here. These mostly apply to key executives, many of whom have the opportunity to take independent advice.

Options and risk

Okay, so you piled everything you could afford into an SAYE, and made a bundle by exercising those options to buy stock in your employer at a discounted rate. The moment those options become shares, your risk profile has changed. You already had a job and a pension through your employer. Now a good chunk of your savings hinges on the prospects of that organisation too. At this point it might be sensible to start to diversify your exposure, even if your company's prospects appear sunny. That applies to shares transferred to a SIPP as well as those outside. Although not much is likely to happen to your pension even if your employer goes bust,[18] you may well lose your job, and your shares (whether inside that pension or not) may be worthless.

There are ways of dealing with the risk. If you find you have several times your annual CGT limit in gains, it certainly would make sense to sell enough to use your annual exemption (£11,000 2014/5) to the full. There are usually other attractive investments out there, and you can reinvest your gains. If you know your industry well, you might even be tempted to reinvest the proceeds in your firm's most capable rival, which would help bolster your savings against competitive risk.

It is quite tempting as an employee to rely on your knowledge of how well a company is doing, but it is not possible to know all the risks. It takes the hard work, often of many thousands, of employees to make a company succeed. But in the days of globalisation, hacking,

---

18   There are exceptions, particularly for firms with very badly underfunded pension schemes, as was mentioned in chapter 4. All employees should make themselves aware of the financial position of their company pension fund.

and fast computer systems it is clear that the foolish or fraudulent action of just one employee is enough to bring a firm to its knees. Anyone at Barings can testify to that.

Conclusion

Employee share option schemes are manna from heaven. I'm only surprised that a sizeable minority of employees find reasons for *not* subscribing, often because they don't like the company or their own manager. This may be cutting off your nose to spite your face. Besides, in most cases you don't have to take the shares at the end, but you will get good interest.

CHAPTER 17.

Taming Taxation

Introduction

TAX PLANNING IS THE STREAMLINING ON YOUR INVESTMENT vehicle. It doesn't do much when you are moving slowly, but it can save you a fortune when you really put your foot down. Never forget it is not the streamlining but the engine – your underlying investment performance – that gets you from A to B.

There are two poles of opinion on taxation. Either it is an essential way for us as a community to finance the services such as schools, hospitals and roads on which we all depend, or it is an unwarranted theft of our hard-earned cash by successive profligate governments. Most of us oscillate between the two views depending on whether we are waiting for an operation in an underfunded NHS hospital, or finding that the plumber's quote didn't include VAT and that we have to pay an extra £12.

Whether you are an investor or not, tax need never be a nightmare if you follow a few simple guidelines:

- always keep records of your income, investments and spending

- don't throw those records away, even after a year or two

- consider the tax implications of any investment or saving decision

- forecast your tax bills and put the money aside

- act early

- HMRC staff are there to help, and free – use them!

Keep records

Keeping records is clearly common sense, but it is amazing how many of us don't do it, or don't do it well enough. The tax system is a slow but precise machine that will dole you out allowances and refunds and all sorts of breaks so long as you feed it the right pieces of paper. Occasionally it might make a massive mistake, which you can only solve if you can show it the correct pieces of paper, perhaps from several years ago.

The national insurance system, a related but even slower machine, needs fewer pieces of paper but if anything these are even more important. If you cannot show that you paid NI contributions on one job you did for only a couple of years in say 1973 you may lose the right to pensions or benefits worth thousands.

Even if you are on pay-as-you-earn (PAYE) and never have to fill out a self-assessment form (lucky you!), you need to keep payslips, bank statements, cheque book stubs, credit card and hire purchase statements, and numerous annual tax forms. From your savings you will receive tax-paid vouchers on which you may be able to reclaim money. Don't just jam them all in a dusty drawer. Buy a cheap concertina file with ready-labelled compartments and start filing. Like so many of these tasks it is horrible to contemplate, but not too bad to actually do. You can even do it while listening to music or watching television.

A few minutes a month filing away those pieces of paper now can save you hours of anguish later on when you can't find the piece you need. Of course, you shouldn't just stuff any old pieces of paper into this file, because it would soon be in as chaotic a state as any drawer. You should also regularly evict those that are no longer relevant or current. Bulky payslips and bank statements can be bundled by tax year, and then put in a box file. If you reserve your concertina file for current paperwork, it all looks more manageable.

Investing records

Once you begin investing, a veritable torrent of paper will start pouring from your letterbox, and emails into your inbox, but only when you have climbed up into the heady heights of capital gains tax (CGT) will any real extra work be required. To incur CGT in 2014/15, your taxable gains must exceed £11,000.

Otherwise, the main chore is accounting for dividend income. Most brokers make this easy by preparing an annual tax statement of dividend income ready to download by June or July, covering the tax year just ended. Adding this into your tax return takes all of two minutes.

Consider the tax implications

Tax is sometimes the defining motivation behind an investment. No one would use an ISA with its dealing costs and annual charges if they didn't expect to recoup the money from eventual savings on CGT, nor would anyone bother to go through the legal expense and complexity of setting up an offshore trust if it wasn't going to save money. Investors in UK government bonds (gilts) need to choose the type with a balance of capital and income return that suits their own tax situation (see chapter 20).

However, don't be seduced into making an investment purely because of its tax advantages. It is far better to pay 40% tax on gains from an investment that is growing in value by 15% a year than to have all gains exempt on a scheme that returns 4% or 5% a year. Cunning tax planning alone will never multiply your money. For that you must invest consistently and successfully. To revisit the metaphor that began this chapter: your investment vehicle, however tax streamlined, needs a decent engine to take you where you want to go.

Forecast your tax bills

For those who are self-employed, and for anyone who pays most of their tax under self-assessment, the long delay between the end of the tax year and when the bill has to be paid at the end of January can lull you into forgetting your taxes. By then you may have spent the money, or it may be tied up. It can be a great mistake automatically to reinvest the proceeds of profitable sales when you have a tax bill looming. Nothing is worse than having to sell a great stock for a pittance in a bear market just because you forgot to set aside cash for taxes.

Using a spreadsheet it is pretty easy to keep a running total of taxable gains, but even those investors without access to a computer should spare an hour towards the end of a tax year in February or March, and sketch out what the tax bills are likely to be. You will already know what you have sold so far, and whether, overall, you did well or not. Any losses should not be forgotten either, as these can often be set against gains. Sometimes you can crystallise losses that will save you a great deal of money, without actually liquidating your investment position (see tax strategies, below). By considering the tax position while the tax year is still running, you have a chance to tweak your tax liabilities, particularly in relation to CGT. If you don't even look at your taxes until the next tax year, you have lost that opportunity.

Once you have a good idea of your tax position for that financial year you will know roughly how much, if any, to set aside. Be conservative in deciding that amount, by setting aside a little more rather than a little less. This is especially important if you will be preparing your own return, because it is so easy to make mistakes.

Act early

The earlier you begin to think about taxes, the more effective the various remedies are likely to be. This is as true for the taxes you have to pay every year as it is for those once-in-a-lifetime events such as inheritance tax.

Your tax office is a resource: use it

Once, many years ago, I went on an Alpine walking holiday. The two most jovial and amusing people in the group were two Cumbrian women in their late 30s, who knew at least as many bad jokes as the men, and could certainly hold their own at the bar. After about a week, when everyone was thoroughly relaxed under the Swiss starlight, the campfire conversation had moved from talk of children, jobs and relationships, right through to divorces and love affairs. When the moment of self-revelation was at its peak, one of the women – I shall call her Valerie – exhaled deeply and looked up, then said: "Here's my little secret. I'm a tax inspector."

You can forgive those who work at HMRC their paranoia when you see hundreds of newspaper articles every week about 'beating the tax man' in some scheme or other. Only traffic wardens seem to reach higher in the scale of those we are encouraged to despise. I see it very differently. These people are only doing a job that needs doing. HMRC is under a duty to levy the right amount of tax, not the maximum possible, and none of its staff works on commission. They actually do a pretty good job, considering the waves of finicky new tax rules dropped on them every year. The abolition of local tax offices in the last year has been a grievous blow to the local service that we used to be able to get, but even the harried staff at the big call centres will be helpful if you give them a chance.

Income tax and investment

Those whose income falls below the threshold for the standard income tax band lose out on investments that pay their dividends net of standard rate tax. These include certain National Savings products, though there are many which pay gross and others, such as ISAs and Premium Bonds, whose returns are tax free. Investors who pay no income tax at all lose out on share dividends, which have a non-reclaimable 10% income tax deducted at source. Those on standard income tax of 20% have no more to pay, while those on higher rate tax of 40% (or 45% for those earning more than £150,000) will pay tax on top of this to bring it up to 32.5%.

For 40% rate taxpayers, the rule of thumb is that you will receive net of tax three-quarters of the net dividend declared, or roughly two-thirds of the gross dividend. For example, if your shares earn a net dividend of 9p per share, the gross dividend is 10p, and after declaring your dividend income you are actually going to receive 6.75p.

Those who pay higher rate income tax, but are below the CGT threshold, will prefer to take their return in the form of capital growth rather than income. There are several options to achieve this end, each with a different risk structure:

* growth stocks

* growth-focused unit trusts or investment trusts

* capital investment bonds[19]

* index-linked gilts.

---

19   It is worth noting that guaranteed equity bonds (GEBs), which seem like capital-generating products, are actually taxed as income.

Capital gains tax

CGT is a tax on the increase in value of assets during your period of ownership. For basic-rate taxpayers it is charged at 18%, and for higher-rate at 28%.

For 90% of people the only asset in their lifetime which would take them into the CGT tax bracket is the home they live in and, fortunately, owner-occupied homes are exempt. Apart from shares and stakes in private businesses, the only other assets you are likely to have which may attract CGT are buy-to-let properties and second homes. The tax issues of these are dealt with in chapter 19.

For the purposes of this chapter I am going to assume we are dealing with the results of share ownership. At its most basic, CGT is a simple tax to understand, but the various frills added in recent years to account for the effect of inflation on assets, and to encourage long-term investing, have had the effect of turning CGT into the ultimate tax monster, in some cases too complicated even for the professionals to understand. Do what you can to keep it simple at your end and there is less chance of having to call for expensive professional help.

Even quite substantial investors can keep CGT at bay for many years when the full CGT allowance is used regularly. As an example, assume an annual investment of £30,000, and an 8% annual increase in value, with profits taken each year and then reinvested. This scheme takes eight years to breach the current CGT barrier, but if the allowance is indexed, as they usually are, it could take years longer. Given the chance to shift the proceeds of sales into a SIPP or an ISA each year, the steady investor is unlikely to be caught by CGT unless she's already wealthy, neglects the basic preparations, or is forced to sell substantial assets in one lump from non-tax protected accounts.

Capital gains tax and your tax return

The first thing to notice is that anything, apart from a home, that you have sold in any tax year, whether you made any kind of profit or loss on it, must be declared if the proceeds (the gross receipts of the sale, not the gain) exceed a threshold twice the size of the allowance. This isn't going to be taxed unless you have separately exceeded the gains threshold.

As far as shares or funds are concerned, your gain is the proceeds at sale, minus the cost of purchase, including stamp duty. Dealing charges for both sale and purchase are deducted from your gains. If you have a computer and can use a spreadsheet, then keeping track is simplicity itself. I find it easiest to add a stock to my spreadsheet the moment I acquire it, noting the dealing cost and stamp duty. This saves hunting through files for the relevant figures when I have made the sale. Even if you don't know how to use a spreadsheet, there are several investor websites that can work it out for you once you plug in your investment figures, dates and overheads.

For those active investors without a computer, a ledger notebook and a bit of self-discipline will save hours when tax-return time comes around.

One thing you will notice immediately is that it is simpler to deal in securities in round and consistent numbers. If you buy 1,000 shares in a company for 150p and sell them all a few years later for 210p, you can work out your gain in your head. But if you bought 1,477 shares and sold 913, then things get a little more complicated. If a few months later you buy back 212 shares and then sell the lot a year after that, you have created a nice little tangle. Add in taper relief or indexation, repeat the operation a few times, and you have created a tax hydra that may need professional slaying. Keep the transactions simple and you keep your taxes simple.

Capital gains tax strategies

There are numerous possibilities to further minimise a CGT bill by using the annual allowance while maintaining the investment that gives rise to it. HMRC's rule that you cannot sell and repurchase an asset within 30 days and crystallise a gain (or loss) has complicated the process of what used to be called 'bed and breakfasting'.

The most commonly used minimisation strategy is to sell a shareholding then repurchase it at the same time within a tax-exempt account like an ISA or SIPP. A related strategy is to crystallise losses in shares that you are convinced are worth holding, but on which you have so far made a loss.

You can offset the loss against your other gains, and because the price is weak you can then fit quite a large number of repurchased shares into your £15,000 ISA allowance. There they are protected against all the upside, that bounce-back in value that you are convinced will come. Of course, losses made inside an ISA or SIPP are not allowable against profits outside!

You can also sell a shareholding, and at the same time set up a contract for difference or CFD (often undertaken by a specialist broker) which replicates that holding, and covers you against price rises. You then hold for 31 days and then reverse the transaction by closing the CFD and buying back the shares. See chapter 21 for more about CFDs and spread betting.

Timing your sales is essential to get the most out of your allowances. However, this should not be done at the expense of your overall investment aims. I have known those who delayed selling at the peak of the dotcom bubble in February 2000, even though they recognised prices were unsupportable, because they wanted to wait for the next tax year and a fresh CGT allowance. By the time that tax year arrived two months later, the market had plunged and gains had been slashed. For at least one of these investors, the cost of that tax strategy was hundreds of thousands of pounds.

Families and taxes

Having a family expands the tax options available to you, but can also make matters more complicated. The principles listed below are not hard and fast, but designed as general guidance. Anyone with a complex tax position should seek professional advice.

- Taxable investments should be put in the name of the spouse with the lower income. However, income taxed only at source can be kept with the taxed partner, who will be no worse off.

- Spouses and children over 18 years are entitled to open ISAs. Encourage them to do so.

- Additional personal allowances are available for widows, widowers, and those separated or divorced who have a child of 16 or older in full-time education living with them.

- Keep the income of a non-working spouse below the tax threshold so bank and building society income can be paid gross, unless the working spouse is a higher-rate taxpayer, in which case it may be preferrable to let a non-working spouse receive investment income above the threshold on the basis that 20% tax at source is better than 40%. The spouse's allowance will be fully used up, and some tax can be reclaimed.

- Those over 65 should be careful to not exceed the threshold income for age-allowance cutbacks (see glossary for allowance details) in case they fall into the age-allowance trap.

- If you are worried about inheritance tax, begin to transfer assets as early as possible to your heirs. Use the annual exempt allowance for gifts and the one-off marriage gift allowance to speed the transfer.

Inheritance tax

Inheritance tax (IHT) is a very complex subject, and many people are surprised that it ends up affecting them. The main reason is that, unlike CGT, it applies to the value of owner-occupied homes. The 2014/15 exemption amount is £325,000, which sounds a lot, but puts many homeowners in the south-east of England firmly within its grasp, especially as it hasn't been uprated since 2009. The rate is 40%, in line with higher income tax bands. Assets passed on inheritance to the spouse are tax-free, and the law now recognises civil partnerships and same-sex marriage in exactly the same way. When the first spouse dies it is important for the executors of the will to pass on the unused allowance to the surviving partner, which effectively doubles the tax-free exemption.

The biggest problems with IHT often begin when the surviving spouse dies, and the children or other heirs have to stump up the tax due before getting a penny of the inherited assets, which not too many people can afford. If you have significant assets to pass on, you should start gradually giving them to your heirs or put them in trust. The first £3,000 a year given away is exempt, and whatever you give on top of that is 'potentially exempt', so long as you live for another seven years. Clearly it doesn't make sense to wait until you are in your 70s or 80s to start! There are also various exemptions for charitable giving and estates connected with woodland, farm, heritage assets and some businesses.

Trusts are extremely useful as they allow you to arrange your affairs to your liking, and they can be used to stop younger beneficiaries getting their hands on certain assets too soon. Trusts don't come cheap in terms of legal bills, however. Starting early makes just as much sense here as in any other aspect of financial planning.

Tax and divorce

Tax may seem like the least of your problems on divorce, but the more money you have, the more likely it is to affect you. The crucial date is the date of separation, not that of divorce. There isn't too much to worry about in income tax, because so much is now done on an individual basis and there is no relief on maintenance payments.

Spouse asset transfers are still exempt from CGT in the tax year of separation, so clearly where any choice exists, patching things up until mid-April in any year will give you both more time! In tax years after separation, assets transferred will be treated as if sold at market value. There can be complications, too, if the husband, as often happens, leaves the marital home, and buys another property before transferring the full ownership of the marital home to his wife. In this case he may be wise to defer switching his principal private residence (where he lives for tax purposes) to his new home until it has been transferred in full.

To confuse matters further, inheritance tax uses the date of divorce, not separation, so spouse transfers have a longer exemption from this tax.

Conclusion

Let us step back from the woods to see the trees. It is important to plan your taxes, to use the allowances which are your right, and to arrange your family's finances and assets in a sensible way. But you must not take your eye off the ball. It is the overall returns from your investments that will multiply your money, not just how cleverly you arrange your taxes.

CHAPTER 18.
Making Money from Bonds

Introduction

THERE IS A PLACE FOR HIGH-QUALITY BONDS FROM GOVERNMENTS and corporations in almost all investment portfolios. This is because of their safety, particularly compared with shares, and their lack of volatility. In the last 20 years, British government bonds, known as gilts, have been one of the best-performing classes of security available, aided by gradually falling inflation and interest rates. Exactly why that helps will be discussed later. But suffice it to say that all good things in markets eventually end, and then reverse. At the time of writing, government bonds aren't particularly attractive for the return they offer, though their security remains intact.

Bonds pay a fixed income. This has led some inexperienced investors to compare bonds with savings accounts because both express the interest income as a percentage, a yield. The two investments are very different. The value of a bond, like a share, can go up or down, while the value of a sum in a savings account will not. Unusually high bond yields, compared with prevailing interest rates, usually tell you something about the balance of risk. Clearly, a 13% government bond issued by an inflation-hit Latin American country or a 9.5% bond issued by a struggling telecommunications company is not necessarily going to make you better off than a 3% savings account from a high-street bank. By the end of this chapter you will:

- understand what a bond is and how it works

- know the different types of government and company bond

- understand the rate interest cycles that affect bonds

- be able to assess the risk and reward on bonds

- know how to buy and sell bonds

- know something about bond funds and ETFs.

What is a bond?

Bonds are a written promise to repay a fixed sum, usually by a fixed date in the future, and usually carrying an interest payment. They can be issued by governments, companies and many other entities, although most of the time they are traded purely between investors. In one sense we are all bond traders already, because the £5 and £10 notes we spend and receive are merely zero-interest Bank of England bonds, promising to pay £5 worth of gold on demand. This has not been a right we can actually exercise since the abolition of the gold standard.

The most important thing to understand about bonds is the relationship between the price of a bond and its yield. Say a company issues a £100 bond which will pay £5 a year for ten years and then be repaid in full. That £5 payment, known as the coupon, is an annual yield of 5% on the £100 spent by the investor who bought it. However, let us say that six months later interest rates in the economy rise and new bonds start to appear with a 6% yield. The original bond still pays £5, and is now up for sale. But no one would offer to pay £100 for £5 worth of annual income when there are opportunities to pay £100 for £6 of income. However, they might offer to pay less than £100, bringing the £5 return to a 6% yield competitive with other bonds. In other words, the price of the bond falls until £5 is 6% of it. That price turns out to be £83.30.

In principle, market forces make a competitive yield for every bond. In practice, however, it is more complicated than the example above. There is the complication that whoever buys the bond for £83.30 will get £100 back for it on repayment, an extra return which adds to the effective yield. The discrepancies between market prices and repayment, and the length of time until repayment are all accounted for in a complex calculation called the gross yield to redemption. This figure is the real yardstick for comparing bonds.

Bonds, interest rates and risk

Bond prices are slaves to interest rates, just as the price of oil exploration company shares bobs up and down with the price of oil. That means that bond prices move not only when interest rates actually move, but when they are expected to, which means taking account of inflation, currency movements and many other economic variables. Those who correctly judge the interest-rate cycle, and buy bonds when interest rates are high but just starting to fall, can make a killing. Buying a £100 bond that pays £15 a year, a yield of 15%, and holding it right down to when interest rates reach 5%, means you have trebled your money. The price to make that £15 yield 5% is £300. Inflation and interest rates are the main risk to the expected value of bonds; the other is the risk of default, i.e. failure to repay or failure to make an interest payment.

The eurozone crisis of 2009–11 and the global banking crisis which preceded it are a timely reminder that the largest banks and even governments can come close to default. While this may not particularly surprise those who look at Argentina (currently in default) or Greece, which has struggled for competitiveness ever since joining the eurozone, it underlines the issue of confidence that lies at the heart of all financial systems. Governments do not actually have to default to ruin the savings of those who own their bonds, it only needs to appear possible that they will.

The same is true of any bond. During 2008, subordinated bonds in many of Britain's banks, building societies and insurers plunged on fears of contagion.[20] Just because it hadn't happened for a long time, doesn't make it historically very unusual. Russian tsarist government bonds from the early 1900s may have seemed a great investment until the Russian revolution, as must Cuban government bonds until Fidel Castro took over in 1958. Bondholders in any of the great corporate bankruptcies of our time probably did no better.

Bondholders may stand ahead of ordinary shareholders in the queue to get a slice of the assets of failed companies, but quite often there is nothing left to share.

Failure to make an interest payment is more common with corporate debt, and doesn't automatically indicate that you may not get your principal back. But it is still a big event, that will damage the value of the bond. There are some newer types of bond, not suitable for investment beginners, called contingent convertibles (CoCo) which are designed, mainly for banks, around the idea of forced conversion to equity in the event of difficulty.

Interest rate/inflation risk is quite different to default risk, and should be treated so. You can diversify to spread the risk of default (and indeed you should) but you cannot diversify away the risk of inflation within bonds. It affects them all to varying degrees.

---

20 I was able to buy subordinated bonds in Aviva, one of Britain's biggest insurers, for 37p in the pound in early 2009, when the 5.9% coupon was worth 16% on the price I paid. In four years I sold them at 93p, having trebled my money, including interest received.

Gilt-edged stock

The great attraction of gilts is for the risk-averse investor, because there is so little risk of default. The only risk is that of interest-rate expectations. While there are dozens of different sorts of gilt, the choice between them is largely governed by the investor's tax status. Capital gains on gilts are free of tax, while interest income is taxed. Therefore the higher your tax band, the more sense it makes to buy a gilt which gives most of its gross redemption yield in capital. The *Financial Times* produces an up-to-date list of the best gilts for each tax bracket each Saturday in the Money section's databank. The government's Debt Management Office has plenty of detail about how exactly the market works on its website. Gilts, like shares, can be bought through a stockbroker or by subscription at issue. Minimum deal sizes tend to be hefty, as do commissions. As many investors require advice on choosing the right gilt, this has tended to be the realm of the full-service brokerage. It is possible, however, to buy individual gilts online through a number of stockbrokers without advice, but you need to do your own research. For most investors, especially the inexperienced, a low-cost fund is the simplest way to access markets for both government and corporate bonds.

Index-linked gilts

Gilts, being purely nominal instruments, are peculiarly vulnerable to inflation compared with shares, which represent real assets. To answer this criticism, index-linked gilts were introduced. They are designed to guarantee a return in line with inflation, in terms of both interest and capital value. They are not too inspiring now, but may come back into their own if inflation starts to rekindle in future years.

Corporate bonds

Corporate bonds are a bit racier than gilts, and a step up the risk ladder towards equities. There is a huge selection on offer, from super-safe but lowish-income issues in huge international companies right through to high-yield issues in struggling companies (see the next section). Like all bonds, corporate bonds are sensitive to inflation and interest rates, but also to the general economic background. Fund routes include both managed funds (watch out for costs!) and ETFs, which are cheaper and cover a wide range even in specialist areas.

If you buy corporate bonds directly you may find it much harder to get hold of research compared with equities, and you should be prepared for a minimum deal size of £10,000, which would make building a portfolio of corporate bonds a massive undertaking. In addition, spreads tend to be larger than on shares in the same companies. All this might explain why only 1% of retail investors' assets are held directly in bonds.

While you don't need to understand a company inside out like you should for shares, you should know it pretty well, and certainly enough to assess its chances of default! Knowing about the credit ratings issued by agencies such as Moody's and Standard & Poor's is also vital, because changes in credit rating directly affect the market value of those bonds. S&P ratings go from the perfect AAA down to BBB for investment-grade risk (i.e. only a negligible chance of default), then there is the separate category of sub-investment grade, affectionately known as 'junk bonds', which offer extremely high yields, but some risk of default.

Junk bonds

When it comes to 'junk' bonds, those in the riskiest but highest-yielding firms, it is pretty much essential to choose a fund or ETF to spread the risk of individual default.

The most popular ETFs trade in the US – which is where most of the constituents issue their bonds – and two well-known ones are the SPDR Barclays Capital High Yield Bond ETF (code JNK) and iShares iBoxx $ High Yield Corporate Bond (HYG), both of which cost less than 0.5% in annual fees. There are dozens of others. Though the investor is well-diversified against the risk of default in such bonds, there are still tidal flows of sentiment to consider. If interest rates rise, they become less-attractive relative to other forms of fixed income, while if recession looms, there will be more defaults. Both can hit prices of these type of funds. Do not fall into the trap of believing that the highest-yielding fund will automatically make you the most money! Just like dividends and shares, bonds and their funds are priced on expectations, which can change.

Subordinated bonds, PIBs and preference shares

Subordinate bonds, PIBs and preference shares are a hodge-podge of intriguing fixed-interest plays, but are worth bringing to the attention of investors. Some of these issues, particularly in insurers, building societies and former building societies, offer a pretty good yield with good security. They are safer than ordinary shares in a given firm or entity, but not as safe as so-called 'senior' debt, the class of bond which has first call on assets in event of a default. The downside is a lack of liquidity which makes bid-offer spreads quite wide, and some complexities in terms of issues that are 'called' by the issuer and then reset at a different interest rate. I have written numerous detailed articles on these, which are beyond the scope of an introductory guide, but can be found online, particularly on the

FT and *Investors Chronicle* websites. Like any investment area, the attractions vary depending on the economic and market cycle.

Bonds as part of a portfolio

One of the great attractions of bonds is that their performance is not closely correlated with shares. Though higher interest rates may hit shares and bonds, and lower ones boost them, most other economic news has a more nuanced impact. Inflation is crueller to bonds, which are nominal assets, than to shares, which are claims on real assets. That alone would justify their inclusion in a portfolio. How much of a good portfolio is a matter of debate. The old adage was that the percentage of bonds should match your age, but that is far too conservative for current extended life expectancies. For those still working, 30% is a reasonable sum – acting as a reservoir of accessible value even when share markets are weak.

Bonds and tax

Bonds listed on any recognised exchange are eligible for inclusion in both ISAs and SIPPs, though ISAs exclude bonds which have less than five years to maturity at time of purchase. Within these accounts, interest on bonds is not taxed. While most bonds pay gross, some fixed interest securities, such as preference shares, usually pay amounts net so you won't get the full benefit. Capital gains are payable on bonds held outside these accounts, except gilts which are exempt. However, most bond funds and ETFs pay their dividends net of 20% tax anyway (not 10% as with shares), so much of the benefit of holding them within a tax-protected account is lost.

Bond funds offer the same disadvantages of any funds: charges eat into performance, and past performance is no use in discerning the future. In addition, they headline whichever of the different yield figures look most alluring. Some with a very high headline distribution yield may be eating into the capital to support it. Don't forget about charges, which afflict bond funds as much as any other.

Conclusion

Bonds have a valuable part to play in a diversified investment portfolio, particularly for those who want income. Never forget that prices go up and down just like shares. For gilts, your tax position and predictions on interest rate movements are the most important considerations. For low-rated or junk company bonds, there are bigger gains on offer, but some risk of default in addition to changes in value brought about by changing interest-rate expectations. Most corporate bonds offer a risk profile halfway between equities and gilts.

CHAPTER 19.

Multiply Your Money with Rental Property

Introduction

RENTING OUT PROPERTY IS A VERY EFFECTIVE, LOW-RISK WAY OF multiplying your money, provided you are willing to make a long-term commitment. There are very few areas in the UK where the value of residential property has not risen in any given ten-year period, and those places, the most depressed inner cities and areas of industrial decline, are pretty obvious the moment you visit them. This chapter covers:

- how to decide if being a landlord is right for you

- timing your purchase to maximise your gain

- understanding the property cycle

- calculating your rental yield

- how to spot problems early

- keeping the tenants on your side

- minimising maintenance costs

- handy tips and hints.

But let's start with the returns. Figures compiled by buy-to-let mortgage specialist Paragon starting in 1996 suggest that the average buy-to-let investment returned 16.3% a year until 2013.[21] That's a staggering figure, which may be related to the fairly favourable starting date. Let's look at the mechanics instead, the gross rental yield, which is the total yearly rent as a percentage of the house value. Those starting now can expect an average rental yield for the UK of 5.5%, from 4.6% in London and up to 6.6% in Yorkshire and the Humber.[22] A decade ago, those figures would have been half as high again, but then so would the cost of the buy-to-let mortgage you would have been financing it with.

Gross rental yield is only part of the potential return, and ignores any capital appreciation. If you are looking at buy-to-let, I would strongly advise setting aside any fantasies about house-price increases. The investment case must first stack up on the costs and returns of providing someone else with a home, something that depends on *your* efforts. The eventual value of that home, which is largely dependent on external factors, should be the icing on the cake. If the first doesn't stack up, don't proceed based on hopes for the second.

Right at the start you should acknowledge that if you buy a flat or house in order to rent it out you are effectively running a small business. This brings bookkeeping, tax, maintenance, legal and safety responsibilities. The law is fairly clear on this point. While for you this property might be purely an investment, it will become someone else's home. As such you need to be prepared to invest time as well as money to make sure you make the right decisions.

---

21   Cited in *Investors Chronicle*, 9 May 2014. This includes rent and capital and involves assumptions about loan-to-value mortgage cover and interest costs.

22   *Money Observer*, August 2014.

Two other non-financial decisions need the closest attention: the quality of the tenants you choose, and how much maintenance the property requires. You are also likely to be investing on margin (if you are buying with a mortgage), without the owner-occupier tax benefits. A long-term view is therefore essential to ensure the long-term rise in property prices works in your favour.

Location, location, location

Location isn't quite everything, but it is always important. There are some peculiarly powerful effects from location which seem to magnify small differences between apparently similar areas. Clapham in south London has been a trendy area for at least four decades, yet Balham, one stop further down the Northern Line, was very slow to move upmarket. Similarly, Brighton is the economic jewel of the south coast, while Hastings, just a few miles east, is still fairly deprived in places. Okay, Brighton has better transport links to London, better architecture, and a less-constricted layout, but they both have the sea and plenty of leisure opportunities. There seems nothing on its own to explain the extent of the difference, except years and years of people pouring their money into one place – not just houses, but restaurants and bars, businesses and education – while neglecting the other. The compounding of small differences makes itself felt, once again.

Many external factors can stimulate an area's value. The extending of fast rail lines to a town, particularly if it links it to London, the building of a major civic amenity such as a theatre or swimming pool, or the hosting of a major event, all have an effect. Bilbao, once Spain's most depressed industrial city, has been lifted to international trendiness by the single act of the Guggenheim art gallery being built there.

Timing

The quality and timing of your investment decision are absolutely crucial. Like a share investor looking for bargains, you will not be alone in seeking the most up-and-coming area, the closest flat or house to a commutable railway station, the most flexible property for improvement. If you are too late in the property cycle then you may have to wait a long time for any capital appreciation – and at worst may be locked in by negative equity for several years. At such times it is also difficult to get the best rental yields, and you lose the benefits of a wide choice among tenants. Once the boom is over, the property on which you are paying a mortgage may remain empty for several months a year unless you want to drop the rent substantially.

While it is tempting to opt for a cheap area when the best areas have become expensive, it is well to remember that this is often a sign of an overheated market. Many areas are cheap for good reasons – poor transport, high crime, lack of shops – and not only are they the last to rise, but almost always the first to fall.

Don't rely on an estate agent to tell you the market is too expensive. While they are pretty good at pointing you to the best areas within their patch, and saying A is better value than B, no one on commission is ever going to give you what might be the best advice: 'Sit on your hands for a year or two. The prices are bound to go down.' It will be up to you to make this decision, and just like being a contrarian share investor, there are gains to be had from doing the opposite of what everyone else is. You get clues to the state of the market from the price indices compiled by the Nationwide Building Society and Halifax. They are only a rough guide, and only to one side of the equation: price. What you are really looking for is indications of affordability; the relationship between average earnings and house prices. It used to be that over the course of a business cycle the average house would cost around three times the average income. These days, with house prices having left median pay behind, it is closer to five times. Despite record low interest rates, mortgage costs which were 20% of average income in the 1990s, are now 30%. What this means is that fewer first-time buyers can afford to buy, unless they have parental help. That means more renting. But it doesn't automatically mean higher rents. Affordability curbs both rents and house prices.

Some more anecdotal measures are appealing, such as what kind of person is buying a particular property. I bought a flat in the London borough of Wandsworth in 1987, just two years before the peak of a housing boom. The people I bought it from were from less-well-paid occupations than mine. When I sold it in January 2000 for what seemed a grand sum, all the prospective purchasers were people far better paid than I, with top City jobs. It seemed to me a good time to be getting out of property, in that area at least, because there would be no one but millionaires who could be the next rung of the buyers' ladder to take the area any more upmarket.[23]

Among my friends is a Welsh artist who has an uncanny knack of living in areas that, though depressed, are just about to go upmarket. He has put his magic touch on Clapham, Wapping, Stepney, and now central Cardiff. In his early years Alun was unable to benefit from his uncanny predictive ability, due to being broke, but now he has made far more money from moving house than from his art, crowned by seeing the value of his Cardiff home quintuple in just over a dozen years. My theory is that struggling artists are the first wave of improvers and gentrifiers, preparing an area for the first of the trendy vegetarian cafés and bohemian bars which so often seem to mark out an urban area for a rise.

Traditionally, British property price movements, up or down, have started as a wave moving out of central London, through the south-

---

23 Well, I wrote that in the first edition of this book, and indeed it was millionaires who moved in next. Properties like mine rose fourfold in value over the next 14 years. Unfortunately, I had already sold!

east and into the rest of the country. A particularly good year for City bonuses filters down as a property price ripple which, together with other indicators of a buoyant economy, wash up on the shores of the rest of the country. Likewise, when City bankers are being fired, London house prices pause for breath, and a wave of weakness washes outwards.

Increasingly, however, London needs to be seen as a separate economy where foreign buying has been a crucial part of the mix, taking up the slack when the bankers flag.

Choosing your tenants

More than any other decision, choosing your tenants will determine whether or not your time as a landlord is a happy one. Bad tenants can make your entire life a misery. They ruin your good relationship with neighbours as easily as they ruin the furniture and carpets. Even if you get your full quota of rent you are unlikely to get much peace of mind. One common problem is for tenants to leave unpaid bills which, even if you don't get chased for, can damage the credit rating attached to the address. If it is your home, you may move back in to find you have difficulties getting accepted for credit cards and other financial services.

Letting agents usually offer a vetting service, but there is no substitute for meeting potential tenants yourself. Your letting agreement (drawn up either by a solicitor or by a standard agreement from a letting agency) should be explicit about your attitude to pets, smoking and sharers. It is also vital that you make a very detailed inventory of all fixtures, fittings, furnishings, kitchenware, etc.

A good face-to-face relationship is as important here as in any business. If your tenants like you, they are much less likely to try to take you for a ride. If you make only reasonable demands from them, then they are unlikely (although there are exceptions!) to make unreasonable demands of you. It pays to give yourself the greatest choice too. If you are not using an agent, make sure you advertise widely. Friends of friends may seem ideal tenants, but occasionally if there is a dispute you may lose a friendship too. If too many of your dealings are done through a solicitor or letting agent there is a danger of formality descending into frostiness in relations. A badly-motivated tenant has more than ample legal opportunity to make life difficult for you.

The financial mechanics

You should certainly know what the gross yield will be before you consider buying a property. If you are in the process of moving out of your home, and are trying to decide whether to sell or let, you should use the current value of your home, not the price you paid, otherwise you don't get a true comparison with what else you could do with the money should you sell.

The difficulty is to turn that theoretical gross yield into a realistic net yield. You may well need to allow for four to six void weeks a year when the property is unoccupied, especially if you are providing short-stay letting for students, or those temporarily in Britain. There are considerable ongoing costs in the mortgage, maintenance, legal bills, letting fees, insurance and so forth. Mortgage interest rates have historically tended to be higher for buy-to-let loans than for home loans, although the entire cost can be offset as a business expense against income. Ironically, since the death of MIRAS, this is no longer possible for residents. There is no equivalent of the ISA to shelter residential letting income. Even SIPPs, which can hold commercial property, are barred from holding residential property.

Tax relief

When you rent out a property you can claim tax relief against:

- the interest costs of the mortgage

- rental insurance

- letting agency fees

- maintenance and upkeep costs

- extra legal and professional advisor's costs incurred after purchase

- a 10% annual allowance for depreciation in the value of furnishings.

Types of property

Accessible choices of property really fall into five types:

1. student letting

2. short-term domestic lettings

3. corporate short lets

4. holiday flats

5. shops with flats above.

Most investors will end up with short-term domestic lettings. Holiday and student accommodation obviously only works in relevant areas, corporate short lets require substantial capital and a totally professional servicing arrangement, while shop and flat combinations can be a little risky for those who are not totally confident in the property market.

Letting to a housing association can be a good option for those who are willing to settle for a relatively low yield in exchange for having most of the hassle removed. Housing associations need affordable properties for workers, such as nurses and teachers, and will take on private rentals in which they, not you, look after all internals. The association will also arrange the letting and guarantee the owner a fixed yield for a fixed period. Flats in former council blocks offer some of the cheapest properties to buy in expensive areas such as London, yet tenant demand means rents can be strong. You may even qualify for an improvement grant.

Student letting can be lucrative in the right areas. The usual plan is to take an old property where large bedrooms or a second living room can be split into additional sleeping accommodation. Further detailed research should be undertaken.

Letting agents

Anyone can set themselves up as a letting or managing agent and, like the population at large, they range from the saintly to the criminal. The Association of Residential Letting Agents (ARLA) can put you in touch with approved firms. Letting agents tend to charge 10–15% of the rent, plus VAT, or they may charge a per-letting fee and a rent-collection fee.

In many cases letting agents run a hands-off approach to maintenance, calling in expensive plumbers or electricians for jobs that are literally a minute's unskilled work when investigated. In some cases they are slow to notice rent unpaid, and if a tenant manages two or three months without paying they may just disappear, being well up on their forfeit deposit.

Many letting agents now offer rental insurance cover, which should protect you against vacant periods as well as non-payment. The premium is a percentage of the rent. Some student-rental properties are not attractive to managing agents because of the hassle factor, so you would have to take a hands-on approach anyway.

Repairs and maintenance

Maintenance is a thorny issue. The better your initial survey and knowledge of the property, the less likely you are to inherit the unexpected problems that lead to continuing large maintenance or repair bills and might affect the value of the property. Those with a practical bent and building experience, and not needing an immediate return, may well like to buy properties needing serious renovation, which can pay substantial long-term dividends but almost always take longer than planned. Others who are willing to settle for lower yields and a quieter life may find modern, purpose-built flats ideal.

If you are prepared for a little DIY, then you can save substantially by doing whatever work is required yourself. My experiences have varied enormously, between doing a Spider-man-style first-floor window ledge walk to deal with a wasp's nest, to an entertaining half hour helping a tenant untangle her underwired brassiere from the drum of the washing machine. (No, she wasn't wearing it at the time.)

Legal problems on purchase

Your solicitor is paid to establish that you are getting what you paid for in a property. Basically, that the seller actually owns what he is selling, that all debts attached to it are discharged on the sale, that a motorway is not about to be built through the front room, that you have full rights to all parts of what is shown in the plan, and that the seller is not going to leave you a loft full of junk that you have to pay to get rid of. The biggest risk, of course, that the place is structurally unsound, is pretty much left up to you to determine. Caveat emptor – buyer beware.

The trouble with this legal process has been endlessly discussed everywhere from wine bars to parliament, but we're stuck with it. A significant minority of solicitors take extraordinary pleasure in devising the most absurd questions to show off their fine legal mind and torture the vendors. When you look at the answers you see that rarely have they moved above the level of school debating points. When I sold a first-floor flat, the buyers' solicitor queried (among literally 92 other things) why the layout plan didn't show where the fences were! This kind of thing causes delay, expense and stress, and in most cases fails to serve the needs of the client. Frequently, most of the really important checking work is actually done by lowly legal clerks, while you pay through the nose for the solicitor's rubber stamp.

Buying rental property

I did my own conveyancing the first time I bought a home, and it was really pretty easy, about six hours' work spread over a few weeks. The hardest part was dealing with the snooty legal professionals from the other side, and having to pay my mortgage lender to duplicate my work. These days, with legal fees substantially lower in real terms than 20 years ago, it probably doesn't pay to do all your own conveyancing, but a bit of common sense can help you learn more than a hundred solicitor's letters.

Try to get the vendors rather than an estate agent alone to show you around the property. If the property you are buying is larger than its neighbours, then some questions should come to mind. Ask who did the improvements and when. Look for second bathrooms, rooms in lofts, extended kitchens and so on. Most will require evidence of meeting building regulations, and those with a window will generally need planning permission on top. In many cases they will not have it. Ask the right questions and you can uncover a liability before even putting in an offer, while your solicitor may not discover this until you are ready to exchange contracts. If you don't see the vendors, ask the neighbours! While you are speaking to them, ask them (diplomatically of course) about disputes, parking, fences and access. Look out for leylandii, those fast-growing conifers which are a frequent source of neighbour disputes.

If buying a leasehold property, make sure your solicitor shows you any maintenance clauses. Some stipulate absurdly frequent redecoration, roofing work, external repainting, and so forth, which can be extremely expensive. At the other extreme, disputes among leaseholders about paying for repairs or maintenance can see property visibly deteriorate while nothing is done. In a block of flats, a great deal can hinge on the efficiency of both the residents' association and the management company or freehold owners.

Shared access is another frequent source of problems: shared drives, shared corridors and staircases, shared garden access. If you let out a converted flat in a shared house, you must make sure the tenancy agreement includes all duties stipulated for common parts, otherwise you as the landlord and leaseholder will be expected to bring your mop and clean the corridor!

General tips and hints

- Choose a property with an entirely pitched (i.e. tiled or slated) roof for low maintenance. Asphalt flat roofs, even if just on dormers or back extensions, need to be replaced every eight years and the first sign that it is required is often a leak all over your careful decorating.

- Failed lead flashings are the most common source of leaks on pitched roofs.

- UPVC windows are lower maintenance than wood.

- Washing machines and dishwashers are best placed on a ground floor where a choice exists.

- Get loft water tanks checked. Make sure you and the tenants know where the stopcocks are.

- If you plan to do the maintenance yourself it makes sense to choose a property that is conveniently nearby. Quite often a job may be trivial in itself, but if it requires 90 minutes each way hacking through city traffic it is going to be a pain. Although receipts for maintenance work can be offset against rental income, HMRC does not usually allow travel costs.

- If you are providing a furnished let, you cannot just get in any old second-hand furniture. Soft furnishings must meet a fire-retardant standard (look at the label). You must also provide a smoke alarm.

- When letting your own home, make sure you inform your building and contents insurer of your plans. If the tenants are to get their own contents insurance make sure that landlords' fixtures, fittings and furnishings are included.

- See chapter 6 for how to get the best from tradesmen.

- You are allowed to deduct 10% of the rent as an allowance for wear and tear when declaring your income. Keep all receipts for maintenance and repairs.

- Buying freehold is the simplest. Where you must have leasehold, try to avoid relationships with local authorities, managing trusts and residents' associations, where all have to approve repairs, communal heating bills, lighting bills, etc.

Conclusion

Renting out residential property to let is a very effective way of multiplying your money. However, it requires a long-term commitment and good judgement, and can soak up a fair amount of time. As a real asset, property and rentals shrug off the effects of inflation, which can make them a useful counterweight to assets such as bonds or cash savings, which are easily damaged by rising prices.

CHAPTER 20.
Margin-based Investments

Introduction

CONTRACTS FOR DIFFERENCE (CFDs) AND SPREAD BETTING are two forms of derivative-based trading, suited only for professionals or very experienced investors, and for that reason they are covered only briefly here. Both methods allow trading of shares, foreign exchange rates, options, commodities, futures and market indices, although examples given here will be only for shares. For those who know how to handle the considerable risks of these very potent instruments, there are several advantages.

Right at the outset, I would like to say that most of these products are designed for and used by traders. That is to say, individuals who attempt to make a profit by keeping a position for a few hours or a few days, and often using chart techniques to try to work out in what direction and how far prices may move. Short-term trading is, on average, a loser's game. Academic studies show what common sense indicates: that a zero-sum game cannot benefit the average participant. Indeed, considering the time spent staring at screens and fretting over positions alone, it will probably cost you money. There is no income to reinvest. There is no GDP growth to lift the value of the securities over such a short timeframe. Like all casinos, the only sure winners are the house.[24] Only those who believe they have exceptional talent should entertain the idea of multiplying their money this way.

Now that's out of the way, these are the characteristics of these derivatives:

- you can magnify your positions for a given investment by using leverage

- you can construct positions that profit from market falls as well as rises

- there is no stamp duty to pay, and some brokers charge no commission

- there is no capital gains tax on spread betting; there is on CFDs, but losses can be offset against gains elsewhere

- sometimes you can trade outside market hours

- they can be used effectively to hedge positions.

Leverage

Leverage, the benefit you get from trading on margin, is the ultimate two-edged financial sword. Say you have £10,000 to invest, and buy 2,000 shares in a company at £5 each. If these rise to £7.50 your investment is worth £15,000, a profit of £5,000. However, if your broker says you only need to put down a 20% deposit (i.e. a 20% margin) on share purchases, you could instead have put a £1 deposit down on each of 10,000 shares for your £10,000 – a five-fold leverage

---

24   And sometimes you can invest in it. There is at least one company, IG, which is listed and which does pay a hefty dividend.

of your original stake – with the broker loaning you the remaining £40,000. If the shares had risen to £7.50, your profit – after repaying the £4 per share you owe the broker – would be £3.50. That means the 50% increase in the share price has magnified the profit on your capital to 250%. Your £10,000 would have become £35,000.

The downside, of course, is that even modest falls can wipe out your capital completely. In the example above, just a 10% fall in the share price, to £4.50, would have halved your deposit and left you with only 11% margin. Be aware that your losses aren't limited to your deposit. You can quite easily be asked to deposit more money to cover a losing position. While setting 'stop-losses' protects against this, they bring their own problems. You will automatically be ejected from positions when a stop-loss is triggered, even if your chosen security later goes on to move in the direction you initially hoped. The money lost on 'stopped-out' positions can soon add up.

Going short

Going short is selling what you do not own in order to buy it back again later at a lower price. When going short you are effectively picking losers rather than winners, as if betting on which horse will come in last in a race. The attraction is that it allows the chance of profiting from falling markets, which gives the itchy trader something to do in those long periods.

In the US it is a widespread practice for investors to borrow shares for a fee from long-term holders such as banks and insurers, and short them, but in the UK there is no corresponding facility, certainly not for small investors. That is one of the reasons why CFDs and spread betting, which do allow you to take short positions on shares, have become popular here.

Contracts for difference

CFDs are traded derivatives which exactly mirror the price of the underlying security, and have no expiry date. An investor buying a CFD in a company share, for example, has the benefits of stock ownership, including dividends, which are funded by the investor who sold the CFD. On sale, all differences in price are settled. Financing can be a major overhead for long CFD positions that are kept open for some time; it is levied daily on the amount borrowed, modified by the cumulative difference in price. The combination of margin and finance costs when a position is running against you makes it clear that cutting losses is an even more important piece of advice in CFD trading than in ordinary share ownership. Going short on CFDs has better financing characteristics because you earn interest on the proceeds of what you sold, although you will have to fund any dividends required.

Spread betting

Spread betting is treated by HMRC as a wager, which is why profits are not subject to capital gains tax (nor are the losses allowable against tax). Otherwise it functions in a very similar way to a CFD. There is a subtle but very important difference. The market making in spread betting is exactly like that in a bookmaker, which means it is based on the gut instinct of the professional making the market and runs ahead to where the market seems to be going. If the market has moved against you it can thus be extremely expensive to get out, and if trading on margin the volatility can be quite frightening.

Hedging strategies

Institutional investors often use CFDs and spread betting to hedge positions, and it is in such uses that their flexibility and speed are a great advantage. For example, a manager of a technology fund in which some stocks have rapidly doubled or trebled might want to sell short some of those holdings that he considers overvalued, or go short on the market indices in which many of those stocks are represented to insure the fund against a feared fall. It is often easier, quicker and cheaper to do this through these derivatives than to sell extensive shareholdings.

Conclusion

This book is pitched mainly at the inexperienced investor and advocates a long-term, gradual approach to multiplying your money. CFDs and spread betting have been included for illustrative purposes and to aid understanding. Clearly, the risk and volatility of CFDs and spread betting make them unsuitable for those without years of experience, nerves of steel and professional levels of skill.

CHAPTER 21.
Ten Common Investing Mistakes

Introduction

WE ALL MAKE MISTAKES, BUT WE CAN ALL LEARN FROM them. If we do that, the quality of our investing and our returns should get better and better. The following are just a few of the most common mistakes:

1. Not being in the market

2. Letting commission sap your returns

3. Taking a short-term view

4. Falling for quick money promises

5. Buying what you don't understand

6. Following the crowd

7. Putting all your eggs in one basket

8. Throwing good money after bad

9. Overtrading

10. Letting it take over your life.

1. Not being in the market

Even if you have only read the first two chapters of this book, you'll know how much you are losing out by not harnessing your savings to the earning power of companies. Even the best savings accounts are left in the dust by stock-market returns over the long term. A study by Barclays Capital showed that £100 invested in a building society account in 1945 kept in until 2013, and adjusted for inflation, would be worth £180. The same money invested in a broad range of shares would be worth £5,140.[25] Enough said?

2. Letting commission sap your returns

How does your car perform with the handbrake on? Not too well, I imagine. The same is true of investments that are saddled with high rates of commission. With-profits life-insurance schemes, endowments, old-style personal pensions and actively managed investment funds do not produce the long-term outperformance required to cover the initial and annual charges that are levied on your funds. If you don't want to invest directly in stocks and shares, using a low-cost tracking fund (with no initial charge and no more than 0.25% annual management charge) will ensure that almost all the market's long-term gains accrue to you, not to a salesman.

3. Taking a short-term view

Don't try to guess which way the market is going day by day or week by week. The market's long-term track tends upwards, and the longer the time scale on the graphs you look at, the smoother

---

25   Barclays Equity Gilt study 2013.

this track appears, especially once you account for all the reinvested dividends. The market is like a stop-start train, and it takes you there at its own pace. You won't arrive much more quickly by jumping off when it periodically stops and running to a carriage nearer the front. If you do, there is a chance of being left at the trackside when it restarts!

4. Falling for quick money promises

You should find good investments – they will almost never find you! There are hundreds of schemes offered to people that promise quick returns. They can be anything from time-shares, pyramid selling and boiler-room scams at the least respectable end, to penny-share investments, savings schemes which offer cash back and free gifts, and endless property-related investments. There are occasionally some decent schemes amongst them, but many more are duds and some are plainly fraudulent. Sometimes old scams turn up in new guises. There are old-fashioned boiler-room scams run on the internet which use chat rooms to stoke interest for stocks that have no prospects of ever making money. The harder the sell, the more persistent the salesman, and the more the scheme is being targeted at the financially inexperienced, the more suspicious you should be. If it is so good, why doesn't the advertisement appear in the *Financial Times*, where those with more money can be found?

5. Buying what you don't understand

Never buy shares in a company you don't understand, however many share tips, bullish articles or gushing tributes appear about it. If you don't understand the products it makes, its market or growth prospects, you won't recognise the signs when things start to go wrong and you may be left holding yesterday's failure. Knowledge is not only the key to making sound investments, it also gives the confidence to retain them when the less-well-informed are panic selling, and to know the correct moment to take profits when the good times are really over.

6. Following the crowd

Investors cannot make money without buying at low prices and selling at high ones. Those opportunities only exist because the investment crowd, with its short-term fixation, is doing the opposite. Contrarians are sceptical of the never-ending market booms, but confident that the slumps don't last forever either.

7. Putting all your eggs in one basket

The investment world is full of the unexpected, and every one of us, however good we think our judgement is, will be surprised by good events such as takeovers or bad ones such as profit warnings. Having a collection of shares in different industries, some money in bonds, and the rest in cash, will give a balance to these risks and rewards, and a smoother upward ride in your overall investments.

8. Throwing good money after bad

Throwing good money after bad is a major mistake, probably responsible for more poor market performance than any other. If a share you own is continuing to fall compared with the broad market, then you must sceptically (and rapidly) re-examine your investment decision, and if you were wrong you must be prepared to sell. If there has been bad news, such as a substantial profit warning, you will rarely regret selling immediately, even if it means a loss of 20%. There is nothing wrong with being wrong – many professionals admit to being wrong almost half the time – so long as we admit it quickly. Even if you are convinced the company is sound, you must never throw in more money immediately. Once a share starts sliding, you may have many opportunities to buy shares more cheaply than you ever imagined. The market overshoots in both its enthusiasm and its disdain.

9. Overtrading

Academic studies of day trading, that internet-related phenomenon where investors jumped in and out of shares for just a few hours, show it was doomed to failure as a strategy, even in markets like the US which have much lower overheads than the UK. For ordinary investors, commission, stamp duty and the cost of your time mean frequent trading will eat heavily into your winnings. It is easy enough to see why. In the long term the market goes up because it is hitched to the economic performance of the engines of the economy. In the short term it can do anything, because gossip, rumours and moods are in the driving seat.

10. Letting it take over your life

The buzz of investing in the markets can be addictive. Widespread access to the internet means that either at work or at home, many keen investors can pretty much stare at share prices all day. This can be anxiety-inducing as well as a waste of time, and it may lead us into two other mistakes which will reduce our returns: overtrading and a short-term view.

Multiplying your money is a long-term idea, and doesn't need to take more than half an hour a week for those with a modest portfolio. Perhaps flick through the financial pages of a quality paper most days, and once a month compare your returns with those of market indices such as the FTSE 100 or FTSE All-Share index. Those with market trackers don't even need to do this much, but those with many shares, or with investments in volatile high-technology stocks, may need to commit a little more time to feel comfortable. Multiplying your money can be a hobby, but once you have started up the process, it doesn't actually require much supervision. Most of its best work is done while you are getting on with your life.

CHAPTER 22.
Conclusion

I F MULTIPLYING YOUR MONEY IS ALL SO EASY, WHY AREN'T WE ALL millionaires?

The truth is that many thousands of ordinary people have made lots of money from long-term investing, but it isn't easy. In fact it is hard. But the hard parts are nothing whatever to do with stock-market knowledge, being familiar with companies, or knowing how a unit trust is constructed. After all, we have seen that with low-cost tracking investments you can get solid, market-average returns with no market skills or knowledge whatsoever. The only difficult parts are finding the tenacity to stick with it through thick and thin, to keep squirrelling away money, and then putting it to work hard for you, year in, year out, for decades at a time.

The most difficult time of all is when the stock market has been falling for month after month, and the papers are full of doom and gloom about the prospects for companies. It is a sad fact that it is at just such times, when ordinary people decide that investment is not for them after all, sell up, and take their losses, that the markets are secretly offering the very best bargains. When the market is at rock bottom, the only way to go is up. You won't read too much about it in the papers or in analysts' reports, because they are creatures of the herd. When shares prices were soaring close to the peaks, they urged us to buy. Only now, when they have fallen to bargain levels, do they urge us to be ultra-cautious. Everywhere I have looked during bear markets, I have seen articles saying we should stay with cash or low-risk bonds. Where were these articles when the market was dangerously high? After all, if you want to avoid a hangover, you switch to water in the last half hour of the party, you don't wait until the morning when the headache is already throbbing!

You need courage and self-discipline to multiply your money. None of us is ever going to get every aspect of it right and the learning process is one that never ends. But starting saving early, not stopping, and making sure those savings work hard for you are three keystones. Easy to decide, sometimes hard to stick with, but available to anyone from any walk of life. In the process, you will have tackled debt, avoided commission-hungry salesmen, and cemented your financial independence.

For those that want the extra edge of performance and choose individual shares, there are lots of exciting possibilities. There is never any hurry about it; beginners will rarely regret following shares in a paper portfolio until they feel confident to take the plunge. In your entire share-buying career, you only need to find a couple of good growth stocks and stick with them, and you will do well. Let those profits run and work quickly to cut losses elsewhere. Always be on the lookout for opportunities – those stocks which you know are good, but which are fully priced 99% of the time. You can be there for that 1%.

Almost all of us have spent our lives in jobs alternating between satisfaction or misery, getting up in the dark in the winter to squeeze on a train with thousands of others, or sit in traffic jams. Why do we do it? We are forced to work, of course, for money. Now it is time for money to work for us.

GLOSSARY

accretive

*A term usually used about takeovers, in reference to the forecast improvement on earnings per share (contrast with **dilution**).*

acquisition

When a company purchases part or all of another. Usually a smaller event than a takeover.

active investment management

A system of investment using a manager to try to outperform a benchmark by buying and selling particular investments.

actuary

Someone who examines pension scheme assets and liabilities, life expectancy and probabilities for insurance purposes. An actuary works out whether enough money is being paid into a pension scheme to pay the pensions when they are due.

additional state pension

Formerly known as SERPS and then as the state second pension, this state pension is based on your national insurance contributions and is earnings-related.

additional voluntary contributions (AVCs)

Extra contributions paid by a member to their own pension scheme to increase future pension benefits. Paying AVCs does not normally mean a member will get more from a cash option.

administration

Part of insolvency law. When a company goes into administration, it is operated as a going concern by externally appointed specialists with a view to meeting the demands of creditors without having to go into liquidation. In the US the process is called 'Chapter 11', after the relevant section of bankruptcy legislation (contrast with **bankruptcy***).*

AIM (Alternative Investment Market)

Started in 1995 for small, growing companies, which have less of a track record than those on main London exchanges. Shares traded on AIM are considered both riskier and less liquid.

amortisation

The process of eliminating a debt or other liability by instalment payments (contrast with **depreciation***).*

analysts

Investment analysts who work for brokerages and investment banks are known as sell-side analysts, in that they are advising external clients. Analysts who work for pension funds and insurance companies, and those whose cash is being invested, are known as buy-side analysts.

annuity

A fixed amount of money paid each year until a particular event (such as a death). It might be split into more than one payment, for example monthly payments. Many schemes use an annuity to pay pensions. When someone retires, their pension scheme can make a single payment, usually to an insurance company. This company will then pay an annuity to the member. The money paid to the member is what people usually call their pension.

annuity rate

Compares the size of an annuity (how much it pays each year) with how much it cost to buy.

APR (annual percentage rate)

A standardised way of working out interest costs, which includes all charges. Always check it before signing!

arbitrage

An attempt to exploit perceived market mispricing, often by buying something in one marketplace and selling in another. Shop staff who sell on goods bought with a staff discount are engaged in arbitrage, as are touts selling fixed-price Wimbledon tickets for ten times their face value.

assets

Physical items (e.g. land or buildings) or intangible items (e.g. goodwill) that are owned by a company or person.

balance sheet

Part of company accounts which gives a snapshot of the wealth of a company (its assets net of any debts) at a given moment. Contrast with the profit and loss account, the relationship being similar to that between the level of a bath of water and the rate of flow into it (or out of it, if lossmaking).

bankruptcy

A company that is legally declared unable to meet its liabilities (contrast with **insolvency**).

bear market

Technically a bear market is in force when the relevant stock-market index has declined 20% from its high point, but more generally it is used to describe a prolonged period of market decline. Investors who expect declines are described as bearish. The saying comes from the proverb that you should not sell the bearskin before you have caught the bear, although strangely enough this is exactly what bearish short-sellers do!

bid *see* **takeover**

bid-offer spread

The difference between the price a market maker will buy a security for (the bid) and what he is offering to sell it for (the offer). For stock-market investors, the easy way to remember which is which is that you always deal at the worse of the prices quoted; you sell at the lower price and buy at the higher. The spread is how the market maker makes a living.

biotechnology

A woolly shorthand term now used for almost any small, technology-based company in the life sciences field, particularly if its products and processes are hard to understand and take many years to reach fruition, and if its share price is volatile.

blue chip

A largely defunct term describing a big and supposedly ultra-safe company, with a strong financial position and a good dividend. Named after the highest value poker chip.

bond

A certificate of debt raised by individuals, companies, or governments. It can have a fixed date of repayment, a variable one, or none at all.

book value

The value at which an asset is written into company accounts. Periodic revaluations of property, stakes in other firms, and so on can produce big jumps in value. The book value of a company is the book value of all its assets minus its debts, and is often considered the floor below which its share price should not fall. See **break-up value***.*

book-building

A process undertaken by a lead manager of a company flotation, placing or IPO, in which investment institutions are invited to indicate the prices and amounts of stock they would like to take.

break-up value

The value of a company if it was closed, all assets sold, and debts paid off. Useful to know when you think about buying the shares as it often provides a floor to the share price.

bull market

A prolonged rise in a financial market sometimes lasting for years. Investors who expect rises in prices are said to be bullish.

buyback

Companies buy back their shares either to return money to shareholders (it increases earnings per share by cutting the number of shares over which net earnings are divided) or to signal to the market that management thinks the shares are undervalued. The repurchased shares are either cancelled, or kept for use in acquisitions and takeovers.

capital gains tax

A tax on the increase in value of assets during your period of ownership.

cash flow

The balance of cash coming into and out of a business. It is very different from profitability. For example, a firm that pays all its monthly costs of £1,000 on time but only gets paid the monthly £1,100 owed by its customers in December may have made an annual profit of £1,200, but it has been cash-flow negative on 11 of those 12 months. Cash-flow problems force many more bankruptcies than does lack of profitability.

chart analysis

An investor tool which studies the history of price movements as an aid to investment decisions. There is no doubt that chart analysis can be useful in timing purchases and sales, and thus in getting the best prices, but the claims of some purists that no reference to fundamentals is necessary is hotly disputed.

compound growth

The process by which interest, dividends or debts mount up. The adding of interest at each stage increases the total at an ever-expanding rate. This book is about you using it, not having it use you.

contracts for difference (CFDs)

Derivative contracts which allow investors to take margined long or short positions on underlying securities or indices. Unlike spread betting the bid–offer spread is no wider than that of the underlying security, although gains are taxable.

contrarians

Those disciplined and frequently successful investors who buy when everyone else is selling, and sell when everyone else is buying. As a strategy this has much to commend it.

contribution holiday

A period when an employer's contributions to a defined benefit pension scheme are stopped for a time, because the scheme has more funds than it needs.

corporate bond

A fixed-interest bond raised by a company.

correction

A minor fall during a rising trend of a market. A small rise in a falling market is a rally.

coupon

The interest paid by a bond or gilt, expressed as a percentage of the nominal value (which is usually not the same as you would have paid for it, so the coupon is rarely the yield).

creditors

Those to whom money is owed.

Crest

A computerised system introduced in 1996 to settle share trades without paper.

current cost

An accounting convention which values assets or stocks at today's value. See also **historic cost***.*

dead cat bounce

A temporary rise or rally in a falling market. From the, hopefully apocryphal, observation that although a dead cat thrown from a high building may bounce on hitting the ground, this sign of movement is not indicative of the animal's return to health. Also known as a sucker's rally.

defined benefit scheme

An occupational pension scheme where the pension is guaranteed as a proportion of final salary. It allows the employee a good idea of the size of their pension well before retirement. No annuity is purchased.

defined contribution scheme

An occupational scheme where the future pension will depend on how much is contributed by employee and employer, investment returns in the stock market, charges by the provider, and what annuity rate is available when the member retires. Also called a money purchase scheme.

demutualisation

The process by which a building society or other organisation owned by its members becomes a company and issues shares.

depreciation

*A loss in value of certain physical assets such as a car or a machine over time (compare with **amortisation**).*

derivative

A financial instrument, such as an option, future, or contract for difference, where the price is derived from the market in an underlying security, such as a share, index of shares, or commodity. For example, the price of coffee futures is related to the actual price of traded coffee beans.

dilution

The watering down of existing investors' stakes in a company by issuing of new shares, for example as a takeover currency or for employee stock options.

discretionary account

A stockbroking account that the broker can manage without consulting the customer, and advisable for all those customers whose position of inside knowledge might otherwise draw suspicion.

divestment

The sale of assets or subsidiaries by a company.

dividend

A payment made by companies, usually as an amount of cash per share. Some firms give the option of taking the dividend in the form of extra shares. In Britain dividends are usually paid twice a year, in the US they are quarterly. Reinvestment of dividends – the process of buying more of a particular investment with the income from it – has been the main engine of long-term investment gains.

dividend yield

The dividend divided by the current price of the share, expressed as a percentage.

Dow Jones

Usually a reference to the Dow Jones Industrial Average of 30 large US shares, the most frequently used by journalists of the measures of the US market. The index is named after the company which compiles it. However, most US investment institutions compare their performance against the S&P 500 index, which is more broadly drawn against 500 companies.

drawdown

*The process of taking lump sums from your pension fund. For most people this has been capped, but all this changes from April 2015 (see **flexible drawdown**).*

due diligence

The process of checking the value of any assets you are about to buy; rather like the survey and solicitors' questions prior to house purchase.

earnings

Company profits after all taxes, and available for distribution to shareholders (sometimes still called net profit in the UK).

earnings enhancement

The increasing of earnings per share through acquisition. See chapter 13 for a critique of this as a justification for takeovers.

earnings per share (EPS)

Total earnings divided by the number of issued shares. A critical focus for investors. Any company could, for example, constantly increase headline pre-tax profits by buying other firms using newly issued shares, but the EPS measure would reveal this skullduggery.

EBITDA (earnings before interest, taxes, depreciation and amortisation)

This type of profit is emphasised by those companies which are building assets, for example a railway or a telecommunications network, on which the interest charges and depreciation temporarily (and in some cases permanently) obscure the returns from providing services using those assets.

endowment mortgage

A mortgage using the investment proceeds of an endowment policy to pay off the sum borrowed at one date in the future, while the borrower continues to pay interest on the entire sum borrowed. (Contrast with repayment mortgage.)

endowment misselling

In the 1980s and 1990s thousands of endowment mortgages were sold with high-cost, low-performing investment plans which never had a serious chance of repaying the sum owed.

endowment policy

An insurance policy which will pay out a single amount on a fixed date in the future, possibly to repay a mortgage, or when the policyholder dies (whichever happens first).

equity

Another name for a share. In the property market your equity is the amount by which the value of your home exceeds the debts, e.g. a mortgage, attached to it.

exchange-traded fund (ETF)

An entire basket of securities traded as a single security. Often with very low costs and tax advantages over unit trusts.

final salary scheme, see defined benefit scheme

Financial Conduct Authority (FCA)

The regulatory body covering most financial businesses. It replaced the Financial Services Authority in 2013.

flexible drawdown

The right to take lump sums directly from your pension fund. From April 2015 this will be renamed flexible access drawdown, and for those over 55 there will be no limits on how much can be taken out, though you may still incur tax at your marginal rate.

flotation

A new issue of shares available to the public, often when a private company lists itself on the stock exchange. Now commonly called an initial public offering (IPO).

free-standing additional voluntary contribution (FSAVC)

A top-up scheme for an occupational pension but run by a pension firm. Usually less-good-value than an AVC run by the employer. Many thousands of FSAVCs have been missold.

front running

The illegal purchase or sale by a broker for his own account ahead of the identical order on behalf of a (usually very large) client.

FTSE 100

An index of the largest 100 publicly owned companies listed on the London Stock Exchange. They are ranked by market capitalisation (market value) and the index is weighted accordingly. The FTSE 250, FTSE 350 and FTSE All-share work the same way but cover a successively broader range of companies.

fundamental investing

Looking at the physical factors affecting a market or security, e.g. the supply and demand, the state of the economy, or the company profit records; in fact, pretty much everything except for the history of price movements, which is what chart analysis examines. Sensible investors should take both fundamentals and charts into account.

futures contract

A contract to buy a certain security, commodity or product, at a price already fixed, but delivered and paid for on a particular date in the future. Chocolate makers, for example, use cocoa futures to fix (or hedge) the price of their raw materials into the future. *See also* **derivatives**.

gearing

The proportion of debt to equity in a company balance sheet.

gilts

British government bonds, so called because of the silvered edge that certificates used to have. Now a byword for safety in investment.

golden parachute

Overly generous salary, redundancy, pension, option or stock benefit terms offered to key directors of a bid target company by a hostile bidder, assumed to be in exchange for their recommendation that shareholders accept the bid–offer. A bribe, in other words.

grey market

An informal market made in securities in which official dealings have yet to start.

hedge

An attempt to offset the financial impact of possible future movements in prices of traded securities or commodities, usually through the use of derivatives.

hedge fund

An investment organisation, usually catering only to the wealthy, which has considerable freedom in the types of strategy it may use.

historic cost

One way of measuring the value of assets. It uses what the assets originally cost, but an amount is often taken off for wear and tear *and age. Used in both company accounts and pensions. See also* **current cost***.*

home-income misselling

In the 1980s thousands of pensioners were duped into signing away the ownership of their homes through fraudulent, expensive or unsuitable home-income schemes. Many died before they received any compensation.

home-income plan

A scheme usually set up by an insurance company, offering income for the elderly by releasing some of the value tied up in their homes.

illiquid assets

Those assets which cannot quickly be sold for cash, such as land or plant and equipment.

impaired life annuity

An annuity which pays more than is usual in recognition of the policyholder's diminished life expectancy.

indexation

A link between an index, usually prices or earnings, and a pension, state benefit or tax allowance.

individual savings account, *see* ISA

inheritance tax

A tax paid on a person's estate after death. Inheritance tax may also be payable on some gifts made during a person's lifetime.

insolvency

When a company or individual is unable to satisfy its creditors. Only when a court ratifies this is it known as bankruptcy.

institutions

Institutional investors, e.g. pension funds, insurance companies, unit trusts and investment trusts, which account for the bulk of stock-market assets.

interest-only mortgage

Similar to an endowment mortgage. Payments of interest only are made during the life of the loan, with the amount that would go to repaying capital instead transferred to a savings scheme which should on maturity have grown sufficiently to repay the loan.

investment trust

A company listed on the stock exchange which invests money in other securities or companies.

IPO (initial public offering) see flotation

ISA (individual savings account)

Allows money to be saved in several ways without tax having to be paid on any interest earned or capital gains made.

leveraged buyout

A kind of takeover in which the assets of the target company became the collateral for loans taken out by the acquirer to effect the purchase. The trend reached its peak in the 1980s, allowing 'minnow swallows whale' takeovers, which often ended with companies being taken private but struggling with mountainous debt.

LIFFE (London International Financial Futures Exchange)

A British marketplace for derivatives and options.

limit order

A conditional share trade instruction which requests the broker to deal only within certain boundaries, e.g. 'Buy 200 ABC Plc if it falls below 230p'.

liquidation

The process of selling assets, particularly those of a bankrupt company.

liquid

How easy it is to turn something into cash. A market is said to be liquid when there are plenty of buyers and sellers, so you can always sell quickly without moving the price much.

long

To be long is to own something. The only use of this term is to contrast with being short.

managed fund, *see* active fund management

management buyout

Where a company is bought out and usually taken private by a group of managers.

margin

The deposit on a securities or derivative position, which allows you to control a much larger position by borrowing the rest from a broker.

market capitalisation

The rough market valuation of a company based on the value of its ordinary shares multiplied by the number in issue.

market order

A share trade instruction which requests the broker to deal at whatever the current market price is (contrast with **limit order***).*

merger

A company takeover where the two entities are approximately the same size. In practice many clear takeovers are described as mergers by the firms involved to smooth the sensitivities of directors in the smaller company.

momentum

A style of investing that relies on the direction of movement more than any estimate of fundamental value. Many small investors get badly burned because they do not know how to recognise when momentum is failing.

money purchase scheme, see defined contribution scheme

mortgage protection policy

Life insurance policy which pays off the home loan on the policyholder's death.

mutual

An organisation owned by its members, savers or policy holders (contrast with company). Building societies, friendly societies, co-operative societies and some insurers began with this structure. It has limitations for capital-raising because it cannot freely issue shares, and governance has often been a problem, but by not having to pay dividends it has a theoretical advantage in provision of cost-effective services to members.

mutual fund

A US name for a unit trust.

negative equity

When an asset, particularly a home, falls below the value of the loans taken to buy it.

net book value

This is what an asset originally cost to buy (called historical cost), less a sum for wear and tear and ageing.

nominee account

A share account in which the stockbroker is the registered owner of the shares on behalf of the customer. It simplifies settlement and allows cheaper dealing, but means shareholders do not automatically get the annual report or shareholder benefits they would if they held the certificate themselves.

OEICs (open-ended investment companies)

The only way I can think to pronounce them is oiks. They are unit trusts with a subtly changed legal structure that allows them to sell their services across Europe. The only difference an investor will notice is that there is no bid-offer spread on the sale and purchase of units.

operating profit

Profits after all costs except the balance of interest received and paid, and before corporation tax.

option

A type of derivative contract which gives the purchaser the right but not the obligation to buy (in a call option) or sell (in a put option) certain securities, assets or commodities to the seller at a fixed price (the strike price) by a particular date in the future.

ordinary share

The usual type of share owned in a company, which confers a proportionate ownership of the enterprise and votes at shareholder meetings, but is the last to be repaid if the company goes bankrupt.

overhang

The situation where a share price is depressed because of the impending sale or expectation of sale of a large block of stock. This can happen in privatisations, the maturing of executive options, or after a takeover which was paid for in shares.

passive investment management

A generally low-cost investment method that follows a particular market benchmark or index by mimicking the constituents of that index. The value of a fund using the method should almost exactly track the fortunes of the index involved.

penny shares

*Shares with a low nominal value, usually below 50p. Buying them looks like a cheap route into investing ('Hey! I laid out 500 quid and own 1,000 shares') but it usually isn't. See **bid-offer spread**. These are shark-infested waters for the inexperienced. Often they are bombed-out companies which have fallen from greater heights and about which it is difficult to get timely, unbiased and reliable information.*

pension splitting

When a member gets divorced and the benefits are split with an ex-spouse. These rules may also affect what happens if one of the couple remarries, or they die before retiring.

PEP (personal equity plan)

A now-defunct tax protection for investment, superseded by ISAs.

personal pension

A defined contribution pension scheme, originally planned as a flexible alternative to SERPS, and intended for those whose employers did not run an occupational pension. However, about 2.5 million were missold in the 1980s to people who either should have stayed in SERPS or had better occupational pensions on offer. Personal pensions are still being sold, but with lower cost contracts.

placing

The issue and private sale of new shares by a company. Normally arranged through one or more brokers, and offered primarily to institutional investors.

Plc (public limited company)

A designation to show a company is listed on the London Stock Exchange or AIM. Most other companies are limited (Ltd).

preferred share

A share which ranks above ordinary shares for repayment in case a company goes bankrupt, and in receipt of dividends. Dividends are usually fixed, and the shares tend to be less volatile than ordinary shares.

pre-tax profit

Profits after all costs except corporation tax, but before the payment of amounts to minority stakeholding companies and dividends to owners of preference shares.

price–earnings ratio (PER or P/E)

The share price of a company divided by the earnings per share. It is how much you are paying in pence for every 1p of after-tax earnings, and a vital investor tool because it measures the market's expectations of a company's growth in earnings. A historic P/E is one using already reported earnings, while the more useful prospective P/E is that using forecast earnings, based on the brokers' consensus.

privatisation

The partial or total removal of an enterprise from state ownership, usually by becoming a public company through a flotation on the stock market, but occasionally by private sale.

probate

The process of approving a will.

provision

In company accounts, an amount set aside for liabilities which are expected but which cannot yet be quantified.

qualifying year

A year when somebody has paid national insurance every week. If they have missed some weeks, they can sometimes pay a single amount to make up those weeks. They may have weeks credited for time receiving social security benefits.

rate of return

The percentage of income and capital appreciation in an investment measured over the initial cost of that investment.

real rate of return

As above, but accounting for the effects of inflation. A savings account paying 6% in a year when inflation is 2.5% has a real rate of return of 3.5%.

recession

A contraction in economic activity that lasts for at least six months.

reinsurance

The passing on of a particular risk or part of a risk by an insurer – often a large risk, e.g. the loss of an oil tanker – by taking out an insurance policy with another company.

reinvestment

The process of using the income from an investment to buy more of it.

repayment mortgage

Payments made are used to repay both capital and interest over the course of the loan. (Contrast with **endowment mortgage**.*)*

rights issue

The issue of new shares to investors at a fixed proportion to their existing holdings. So a 1 for 4 rights issue would mean the investor could buy one new share for every four already held. (Contrast with **placing**.*)*

risk

The everyday definition is of the chance of an adverse event occurring, but in investment it often means the likely deviation from expected returns, both above and below the average. (Compare with **volatility**.*)*

self-invested personal pension (SIPP)

A pension plan where the member decides the scheme's investments, or employs someone to advise. Originally for the wealthy, some lower-cost schemes are now being offered through stockbrokers.

share

A document conferring part-ownership of an enterprise, see **ordinary share**.

shareholder value

A concept of the value of a business, based not just on the fundamentals of good management, market position and rising profits, but in circumstances like a takeover, which rival proposal would make most money for shareholders.

share split

The dividing of existing shares into smaller units with no effect on issued share capital. The main function of a share split is psychological, based on the assumption that investors prefer to hold 1,700 shares worth 169p each than 17 shares worth £169 each.

shorting or going short

A short position is selling something you don't have in order to profit from an expected price fall before you have to buy it back. A simple bear necessity, you might say.

short interest

The total value of all short positions in a share or security.

split capital investment trust

A hybrid investment vehicle with a fixed winding-up date offering several classes of share tailored to the tax needs of investors, whether it be pure income, pure capital gains or anything between.

spread betting

A flexible type of margin-based derivative. Investors can buy or sell a security or index through a hybrid contract, and provide a margin against adverse movements. This and the ability to go short are the main attractions. Because deals are constructed for tax purposes as wagers, gains are free of capital gains tax. (Compare with CFD.)

stakeholder pension

A low-cost, flexible pension, which can be taken as a personal pension scheme or a defined contribution occupational pension scheme.

stamp duty

Tax paid on a sale of property or shares. For shares the rate is 0.5% of the securities bought; for homes there is a banded scale, which accelerates sharply on purchases over £250,000 with increases covering the entire proceeds, not just the marginal excess as it would in all other taxes.

state earnings-related pension (SERPS), see **additional state pension**

state second pension, see **additional state pension**

stock

Another word for share.

stock dividend

A dividend option which gives shareholders the chance of receiving the dividend in the form of shares instead of cash. Sometimes called a scrip dividend.

superannuation

A term used mainly in public-sector occupational schemes to describe a member's contributions.

takeover

The process by which one company buys another either with shares, cash or a combination of the two. See also **merger**.

tax avoidance

The wholly legal process of arranging your tax affairs so as to minimise the tax payable. This would, for example, include making sure you fully use all allowances to which you are entitled.

tax evasion

A criminal act. The deliberate misreporting or omission of financial details for the purpose of defrauding HMRC.

ticker symbol

US term for the share code of a company or fund.

top-slicing

The gradual sale of a successful investment.

tracker fund

A passive investment fund that mimics a particular index or benchmark by investing in the constituent securities in that index. A FTSE 100 tracker would hold shares in the 100 constituent companies in that stock.

trust

A legal entity which allows assets owned by one set of people, or beneficiaries, to be managed and run by others, known as trustees.

underfunding

When a pension scheme's assets are less than its liabilities.

unfunded scheme

A pension scheme in which today's pension benefits are paid from contributions levied on today's non-pensioners. Investment plays no part. The state pension system and some public-sector schemes such as that of the police work in this way. SERPS is a type of unfunded scheme.

unit trust

An investment fund in which investors can buy units, and the funds received are invested by the fund manager. The price of the units depends on the performance of those investments. (Compare with **investment trust**.)

vested rights

The benefits for an existing pensioner, or preserved benefits for deferred pensioners, or benefits an active member can have unconditionally on leaving the scheme.

volatility

The statistical variability of a security or index from its long-term average price. For example, the prices of shares in dotcom companies have been extremely volatile while the prices of gilts have not.

warrant

An option to buy a stock issued by a company, often coupled with a bond in that company. Warrants usually have a fixed expiry and a fixed price. (Compare with **traded option**.)

winding up

The liquidation of a company, trust or investment scheme, or an occupational pension scheme. For a pension scheme it can one by buying annuities for all the members, or deferred annuities in some cases. Another way of winding up a scheme is to move all its assets and liabilities into another scheme. This will be done by following the scheme rules, or any laws that apply.

with-profits policy

Now largely superseded, with-profits is an insurance policy that offers a policyholder a share of any surplus in the insurance company's life insurance and pensions business. Criticised for its opacity and high charges, and many cases of misselling. (See **endowment mortgage**.)

workplace pension

This replaced the stakeholder pension as a workplace scheme in 2012. It is the government's safety net for employees, an attempt to build in the savings habit amongst the many low-paid and part-time employees who often don't get round to building a pension. Every employer must enroll any UK employee who is at least 22 and earns at least £10,000 a year.

INDEX